SNOW LEOPARD

Snow Leopard

STORIES FROM THE ROOF OF THE WORLD

EDITED BY DON HUNTER

UNIVERSITY PRESS OF COLORADO

Boulder

Published by University Press of Colorado
5589 Arapahoe Avenue, Suite 206C
Boulder, Colorado 80303

The University Press of Colorado is a proud member of
the Association of American University Presses.

AAUP 1937 / 2012

The University Press of Colorado is a cooperative publishing enterprise
supported, in part, by Adams State College, Colorado State University, Fort
Lewis College, Metropolitan State College of Denver, Regis University,
University of Colorado, University of Northern Colorado, Utah State
University Press, and Western State College of Colorado.

∞ This paper meets the requirements of the ANSI/NISO Z39.48-1992 (Permanence of Paper).

Library of Congress Cataloging-in-Publication Data

Snow leopard : stories from the roof of the world / Don Hunter, editor.
    p. cm.
  Includes bibliographical references.
  ISBN 978-1-60732-193-4 (cloth : alk. paper) — ISBN 978-1-60732-205-4 (ebook)
  1. Snow leopard—Anecdotes. I. Hunter, Don O., 1951–
QL737.C23S582 2012
599.75'x55—dc23

                        2012019778

21 20 19 18 17 16 15 14 13 12   10 9 8 7 6 5 4 3 2 1

"Kashmir" and "Magic Valley" by Helen Freeman. © 2005 by Helen Freeman.
Printed by permission of Stan Freeman.

"Death of a Bharal" by Mitchell Kelly. © 2010 by Mitchell Kelly. Printed by
permission of the author.

"November 13" by Peter Matthiessen. © 1978 by Peter Matthiessen. Printed by
permission of the author.

"On Meeting a Snow Leopard" by George B. Schaller. © 1972 New York
Zoological Society. Printed by permission of the author and courtesy of
Wildlife Conservation Society.

Dust jacket design by Daniel Pratt and Logan Hunter

To Helen Freeman and Rinchen Wangchuk.

Their voice for the snow leopard
inspired many and continues to echo
in the great mountains of central Asia.

CONTENTS

CONTENTS

CONTENTS

FOREWORD: OUT OF WHITE

The most charismatic of the great cats may have seen me in the wild, but I have not seen it, nor do I ever expect to. All my snow leopard paintings have been based on animals I observed in zoos. Though I have never seen a snow leopard in the wild, I have ventured into its mountainous world. My wife, Birgit, and I accompanied Helen Freeman, founder of the Snow Leopard Trust, to the edge of snow leopard country in the Himalayan region of India, Sikkim, and Nepal. Over the years, we have gotten to know Rodney Jackson and become close friends with Peter Matthiessen, two of the contributing authors to this moving collection of essays. Their stories, along with the others in this book, exemplify the personal connection between a rare cat and the scientist-explorer drawn to study and protect it.

Hermann Hesse wrote in his novel *Narcissus and Goldmund* that "true art must have a sense of mystery." It is likely that my artistic fascination with the snow leopard comes with its innate sense of mystery. Also, I have a love of muted colors. The subtle variety of grays in this cat's fur has far more appeal to me than the vibrancy of a scarlet macaw. Darkness is associated with mystery, but so are mist and whiteness. In the painting *Out of the White* I was feeling a hope that snow leopards are emerging into a brighter and clearer future.

Just recently, we once again traveled the high roads of snow leopard country, enjoying the beauty of Ladakh's iconic monasteries and watching blue sheep graze on steep mountainsides. We saw no snow leopards but sensed their presence, feeling lucky and thrilled to be under the distant gaze of this magnificent cat. May you experience a similar feeling as you read about the snow leopard in this remarkable collection.

ROBERT BATEMAN

PREFACE

The idea for *Snow Leopard: Stories from the Roof of the World* came from reading Marc Bekoff and Clara Blessley Lowe's *Listening to Cougar*, an anthology of personal communion with the big cat of the western United States. The inspiration for this book came from my internal voice calling me to tithe in return for a spirit enriched by sharing time and space with the cougar's cousin in central Asia. Unlike the cougar, very little has been written about this beautiful and mystical cat, especially at an emotional, personal level. The world's coolest cat is in deep trouble, its world under siege. To survive it needs empathy, it must roar, awakening an unknowing world. But this big cat has no roar—the only big cat that doesn't. This unique anthology speaks out on behalf of the cat with no roar. It attempts to give a voice to the snow leopard, a voice that transcends species, a voice echoed by those who know it best: the rare few who have given a portion of their lives to help preserve this beautiful cat.

I've carefully selected contributors who truly know the snow leopard, having paid the price of priceless time in the world's mightiest mountains. Most of them are friends and colleagues I've traveled with, worked with. These good and hardy people share a common passion for protecting the snow leopard and its fragile world. I've shared their experiences, heard their stories; I know they will inform, inspire, and imbue readers through heartfelt stories of adventure, danger, and discovery. *Snow Leopard: Stories from the Roof of the World* brings these journeys to life, shared in every detail by a breed of scientist-peregrine as rare and tough as the cat they study.

There is an art to quests of science and spirit. Raw experience without perspective and inner reflection is empty of meaning and does little to shape the core of who we are. In this sense, the nature and depth of adventure are attenuated through prisms of individual self: what's adventure to one person may bore another, and vice versa. Central Asia possesses a timeless magnetism for the adventuresome sprit. Long before I set foot in the great mountain ranges the snow leopard knows as home, a league of extraordinary people marched the river trails and crossed the high passes, lifting the veil of the unknown. These early travelers shared a common pathology of spirit, shamelessly addicted to high remote places, seeking kinship among strange faces, and finding solace in endless horizons. They veiled their passion beneath quests of religion, trade, health, conquest, science.

Earlier scientists and adventurers wrote eloquently of their exploits. These seminal artists of words spawned an entirely new genre of evocative prose, engrossing the armchair traveler with voyeur glimpses of exotic lands heretofore known only as terra incognita. Marco Polo, Ibn Batutta, Hsuan Tsang, and Sven Hedin are but a few who found snow leopard country alluring, a place of greatness:

> Great things are done when men and mountains meet;
> This is not done by jostling in the street.
>
> —WILLIAM BLAKE, *GNOMIC VERSES*

Blake would have us believe such discovery of place and spirit happened only among men, but, in fact, many astonishing women were also drawn to the adventurous life, rebuking the easy path of "jostling in the street." Overcoming repressive restraints of sex and Victorian decorum, which men did not have to deal with, these amazing ladies possessed a deep well of grit equal to that of any man, racking up feats of discovery hardly believable if their exploits were not so well documented. Further, they did so throughout their lives: Fanny Bullock Workman was a record-setting mountaineer at fifty-three, Alexandra David-Neel at fifty-six walked 2,000 miles across the Tibetan Plateau to reach Lhasa, and Isabella Bird in her seventieth year capped an illustrious life of adventure with a 1,000-mile horseback trip through Morocco. Bird climbed Longs Peak in Colorado and traveled around central Asia well over a century before me. I'm very proud that three equally intrepid women have stories in this book, continuing a legacy that proclaims the world of the snow leopard forever genderless.

With all great adventures there are risks, hardships, and unexpected bends in the road. H. W. Tilman was almost apologetic about writing of his unsuccessful attempt on Mount Everest in 1938, for he felt so much had already been said about the great expeditions. But his journey, his epic tales, joined many other stories written about this remarkable region, reaffirming a style for discovery marked with honor and purpose. Some say the great discoveries, great expeditions, true adventure are a thing of the past, that every nook and cranny of the earth's surface has been mapped, photographed from space, and otherwise probed like a hospital patient. I say the great adventures are not over but have merely taken on new dimensions. For an ecologist, central Asia's vast mountains are inhabited by rare species barely studied. Unlocking the secrets of species such as wild yak, black-necked crane, Tibetan antelope, argali sheep, markhor, ibex, kiang, and the snow leopard plumbs the heights of adventure. Just to ply the same trails and mingle with the spirits of past greats such as Hedin, Sir Francis Younghusband, David-Neel, Polo, Joseph Rock, and so many others is adventure at its purest — explorers of mind and place drawn to the great mountains, the quiet places, by forces that transcend generations. The authors of this book are kindred spirits whose souls are fed by purpose in the high places. They include the sage pioneers of snow leopard research and a cadre of younger ones who keep hope alive for future generations. They tell the story of the snow leopard from the roof of the world.

ACKNOWLEDGMENTS

After reading *Listening to Cougar* by Marc Bekoff and Clara Blessley Lowe, I immediately envisioned a similar collection on the snow leopard, written mostly by snow leopard researchers and in-country wildlife managers. I approached Marc with the idea for this book; he not only encouraged the idea but also put me in touch with Darrin Pratt, director of the University Press of Colorado. Darrin enthusiastically signed on to the project, trusting that I would deliver a book of stories most of which were as yet unwritten. I was lucky to have Marc and Darrin as early supporters. I wish to thank George Schaller and Peter Matthiessen for sharing their early works on the snow leopard. Peter's *The Snow Leopard* first brought the snow leopard into the light of the world and continues to inspire and guide new generations of readers. Snow leopard experts Rodney Jackson and Tom McCarthy helped me finish out my list of authors, including a few younger faces. My sincere thanks to all the authors for sharing their stories and bringing them to life with the warmth of nonscientific prose.

Early in my snow leopard career, Helen Freeman opened her home and her heart to me. Her influence guided me to a long-awaited world, and her friendship helped shape who I am today. Rod Jackson further opened this new world to me as mentor, colleague, and friend. Rod's and his wife Darla's Buddhist wisdom and selfless devotion to snow leopard conservation continue to inspire me and many others.

My work and the work of many of my colleagues greatly benefited from the deft support of Dave Ferguson, Fred Bagley, and Steve Kohl in the International Affairs Office of the US Fish and Wildlife Service. The good news about Sheru, a snow leopard pivotal to the chapter "Raising Sheru," came from Dr. A. K. Jha, director of the Padmaja Naidu Himalayan Zoological Park (PNHZP). The PNHZP continues to provide good care for Sheru (Neeta) and nine other snow leopards.

Thanks to Dora Medellin for assembling all the manuscripts into a single, organized text. Mary Greeley, good friend, author, and test reader, provided helpful suggestions and encouragement. I especially thank my sons, Logan, Jesse, and Ben. They encouraged my work abroad and endured without complaint my time away. Thanks also to Carolyn Walter, a friend to all cats, for supporting my cat adventures.

Finally, I would like to acknowledge and thank the local people and families referenced in our stories. The snow leopard's future in the wild relies on the compassion and sacrifice of these good people and countless others like them.

SNOW LEOPARD

INTRODUCTION
GIVING VOICE TO THE SNOW LEOPARD

THE PEOPLE

High in the lofty peaks of central Asia, a rare, elusive cat sits curled on a rocky ledge overlooking a deep, rugged valley. A cold wind wisps frozen snow into the thin air, creating a dazzling silver shower against a brilliant azure sky. It's quiet up high, just the occasional crack of a distant glacier, a few rocks dancing down the shoulders of near-vertical mountains. Across the valley, a herd of blue sheep, the cat's favorite food, grazes peacefully on a steep southern slope. Piercing feline eyes are fixed on nothing but see everything. There are no people in sight, just miles and miles of snow-clad peaks in every direction—a sign that all is well at the roof of the world. The big cat rises contentedly, rubs at the knees of the mountain gods, then disappears. Tracks, vanishing into the snowy mist, are the only evidence it was really there. This near-mythic beast is the snow leopard, the highest mammalian predator and symbol of all that is free and truly wild in the mightiest mountains on earth—its presence, its aura, a living soul given to citadels of stone and ice.

Like no other large cat, the snow leopard evokes a sense of myth and mysticism, strength and spirit. A mystery cat shrouded in a snowy veil, seldom seen but always present. To the West, the snow leopard is a cat of strange, foreign lands, a prowler of high peaks, symbol of survival in the high mountains. To Asia, the snow leopard is embedded in ancient lore and lately has become the symbol of unity and conservation in a region Marco Polo described as "noisy with kingdoms." For local people who share its mountain realm, there is respect and fear. Not personal fear, for the snow leopard doesn't harm humans, but fear of the occasional night stalker that kills precious livestock, the literal lifeblood of existence for those hardy souls who share the snow leopard's world.

The snow leopard is endangered, imperiled by ever-growing human encroachment into its mountainous world. Even with international protection, it is still killed for its bones and luxuriant fur or in retaliation for killing livestock. Climate change adds another dimension of stress to the snow leopard's world, warming the great mountains, pushing the snow leopard and its prey higher and higher. Like the polar bear and Arctic ice, the snow leopard's habitat is sharply defined with no options for retreat or alternative refuge—the balance of life is easily degraded but not easily restored. Beyond the mountaintops lies extinction.

Strangely, the snow leopard ranks high among notable rare animals—alongside the bald eagle, polar bear, lion, tiger, and panda—yet it is perhaps the least studied and certainly the least written about. There is a good reason why we know so little about the snow leopard. Its support system is a delicate veneer of vegetation draped over the highest and most rugged landscapes on earth. And the great mountains are not always a friendly place. For centuries, treacherous travel, rugged terrain, ageless border disputes, and political intrigue have kept this region of the world from indepth study. The seven great ramparts of central Asia present one of the most formidable and foreboding environments in the world. Their names alone evoke a sense of wonderment: Altai, Pamir, Tien Shan, Kun Lun, Hindu Kush, Karakorum, and the mighty Himalaya. Here, in the land where the snow leopard finds comfort, humans can suffer frostbite and sunburn at the same time. Anyone who has traveled in this region will attest that half the enterprise (and half the adventure) is just getting around these impressive giants of the world. When Sir Francis Younghusband crossed the India-Tibet border en route to Lhasa in 1903, his soldiers were supported by 10,000 coolies, 7,000 mules, 4,000 yaks, and 6 camels. Today, border disputes, bandits, bureaucrats, bad roads, and bad weather still persist, about the same as they were centuries ago. The only difference from days of old is the mode of travel; the travelers are the same—adventurers, peregrines, dacoits, seekers. These conditions keep away the less hardy and the faint-of-heart and make the snow leopard one of the most difficult and expensive animals on earth to study.

But extraordinary animals attract extraordinary people. It is possible to study the naked mole rat, monkey-faced mussel, or myriad other creatures without becoming emotionally attached. This is not the case with snow leopards, however. Scientists who work in central Asia are driven by more than just the science. True confessions expose an overwhelming urge to feed twin desires of scientist and adventurer. To study the snow leopard is as much bold adventure as scientific expedition. The high places attract two kinds of adventurous spirits: those who drink in the moment and move on, and those who are moved deeply by an awesome connection with something beyond human description. The latter cannot leave behind only footprints. Their souls would not bear it; they must in some way tithe to the spirit mountains, the spirit cat—in time, deeds, words.

Renowned field biologist Dr. George B. Schaller first saw a snow leopard in 1970 while on an expedition in Pakistan's Chitral Valley. He was studying the Himalayan blue sheep or bharal, a half-sheep, half-goat biological oddity and favored prey of the snow leopard. In the previous twenty-five years, only he and one other westerner had laid eyes on the snow leopard in the wild. He later returned to Chitral in hopes of radio-collaring several leopards to learn about their secretive habits. It was too late. In less than four years, almost all the cats in the area had been shot or trapped for their luxurious and valuable pelts, an all-too-common story throughout the snow leopard's range. In his book *Stones of Silence*, Schaller conveyed his reverence for the snow cat, "a rare and elusive creature which lured me on, only seldom permitting a glimpse." The book's title has become a common metaphor of foretelling should the snow leopards cease to exist.

In his book *The Snow Leopard*, Peter Matthiessen brought this mystical cat out of lore and obscurity into the light of the world. In 1973 he and Schaller set out for northwestern Nepal, near the Tibetan frontier, to again study the bharal and again with hopes of seeing the elusory snow leopard. They spent many months in the Land of Dolpo on the Tibetan Plateau among the people and prey of the snow leopard. The ensuing months yielded only a tantalizing glimpse of the "ghost of the mountain" for Schaller. Matthiessen did not see the snow leopard at all; nonetheless, inspired by the legendary cat and drugged by the thin pure air of the Himalayas, he wrote about their journey. His book revealed much about a man's spiritual search for enlightenment in a land so physically close to the heavens.

Eight years later, Rodney Jackson embarked on the first scientific expedition aimed at studying the snow leopard. His study site, the rugged Langu Valley in western Nepal, was sixty miles from anywhere—truly a *Never Cry Wolf* adventure on the other side of the world. Conducted in terrain hardly suitable for goats, through monsoon rains and the worst winter in Nepal's history, his valiant research established a critical base of scientific data on the endangered cat. Jackson was the first person to capture and radio-collar a snow leopard. He received a serious bite in the process, which almost ended the study before it began. The adventure inspired Darla Hillard's book *Vanishing Tracks*, a compelling story of love and adventure among the endearing mountain people of Nepal and beneath the snow leopard's gaze.

In 1986 Rodney Jackson and Darla Hillard drove an ancient Honda Accord with 220,000 miles on it from Sonoma, California, to Fort Collins. Against incredible odds and hardships, Rodney had just completed the first scientific study of the snow leopard in

Nepal's remote Langhu Valley, high in the Himalaya Mountains. With four years of telemetry data on five radio-collared snow leopards, he had sought me out to help analyze his data using GIS. I was honored to help, and it was a delight to meet Rod and Darla and hear firsthand of their work and adventures in Nepal. *National Geographic* had published their story just before their visit. Although I did not know it at the time, their friendship and influence put legs under a college daydream.

In the many kingdoms visited by Marco Polo, it was tradition for neighboring rulers to lavish gifts — the more exotic the better — on each other during state visits, so rare and unusual wildlife were common in the courts of Asia's ruling aristocracy. The great Genghis Khan had a personal zoo of exotic species collected from or gifted by distant sub-kingdoms. In the 1970s the two noisiest kingdoms were the United States and the Soviet Union, during the height of the Cold War era. In 1972 Richard Nixon opened relations with China and warmed relations with the Soviet Union, launching a period of détente between the countries. China sent the United States two rare and famous giant pandas. Just prior to Nixon's 1972 visit to the Soviet Union, Seattle's Woodland Park Zoo acquired two rare snow leopards from Kirghizia. They were named Nicholas and Alexandra, after the last imperial family of Tsarist Russia.

These two cats fell under the watchful eye of a devoted volunteer at the zoo, Helen Freeman, a serendipitous encounter for both the cat and the woman. As I stated earlier, extraordinary animals attract extraordinary people. Helen spent hours and hours observing the cats and researching what she could about how to care for them. At the time, little was known about them. Her desire to help the new visitors quickly turned to aiding the species as a whole. In 1981 she founded the Snow Leopard Trust (SLT), the first nongovernmental, nonprofit organization devoted to snow leopard conservation. Through the SLT she took her campaign to zoos around the world but, more important, to the countries with the snow leopard. Blessed with a maternal persistence and genuine ease with people, Helen attracted financial support from Seattle's social elite and earned the trust of local village heads half a world away. I

traveled with Helen on several occasions and marveled at her dedi-
cation, passion, and persistent charm. To help the snow leopard,
she changed governments, changed old attitudes, and surmounted
cultural divides. In Peshawar, Pakistan, I saw her genuine passion
and charisma disarm an entire room of exclusively male Muslim
counterparts. This experience taught me to never underestimate
the power of passion or the fact that in some cultures a stone-faced
countenance often hides a compassionate heart.

Her work wasn't without personal sacrifice. Peshawar is a
city where sweltering heat magnifies unabated pollution, horrible
conditions for Helen's rare lung disease. Though weakened and
distressed during our time in Peshawar, Helen never missed a
meeting or complained. She was a quick study of people and the
conditions needed to have a positive effect on snow leopard conservation. Her story "Kashmir," reprinted in this volume, exemplifies the grit, determination, and sense of wonder that was Helen
Freeman. But very little was known about snow leopards when she
started the SLT, especially in those far-off countries with strange
names and people. Helen died in 2007, leaving behind a legacy of
accomplishments that make her one of the great voices for snow
leopards.

Helen was naturally drawn to Rod Jackson, the world's first
snow leopard specialist. Rod and his wife, Darla, helped launch
many of the SLT's early programs before setting out to establish their own institutional voice for the snow leopard: the Snow
Leopard Conservancy (SLC). Focused at the community level, the
SLC promotes local stewardship of the snow leopard and its prey.

In an effort to fill the paucity of data on the snow leopard, Dr.
George B. Schaller initiated a live animal study in Mongolia in 1992,
partnering with Dr. Jachingyn Tserendeleg, director of the Mongolian
Association for the Conservation of Nature and Environment.
Together they began a study in the South Gobi that was eventually
turned over to Tom McCarthy, an Alaskan grizzly bear biologist.
Tom and his team collared and monitored five snow leopards, one
with a satellite collar. This study revealed new information on the
snow leopards' movements and home range requirements.

There have been a handful of other studies on the snow leopard; several are mentioned in the stories that follow. Snow leopards are no less difficult to study than they were in the early years, still requiring a hearty constitution suited to high, cold places. But the way snow leopards are studied has changed considerably, and the number of dedicated organizations has grown as well. Today, new advances in DNA analysis and remote camera trapping point to a promising future in which the cost of studies will become more reasonable and the need to capture live animals greatly reduced — technology intertwined with old-fashioned fieldwork.

To this end, Tom McCarthy returned to the South Gobi in 2008 to set up a long-term research program on the snow leopard. This time as SLT's science and conservation director, he partnered with other organizations to establish Camp Tserendeleg, named to honor Dr. Jachingyn Tserendeleg, who passed away in 2001. The camp is a fitting homage to a wonderful person, an internationally recognized conservationist, and a great friend and voice of the snow leopard. The only active research camp in snow leopard–range countries, it is perhaps fitting that it is in Mongolia where only a little more than twenty years ago it was possible to hunt snow leopards for trophy. Today, the camp hums with the activity of a multinational cadre of researchers and volunteers conducting state-of-the-art research on the snow leopard. A model for other countries, Camp Tserendeleg stands as a vanguard of hope for the snow leopard's future.

NATURAL HISTORY OF THE SNOW LEOPARD

After breaking from Madagascar about 90 million years ago, the India Plate sped across what is now the Indian Ocean, colliding with the Eurasian Plate 40 million years later. The India Plate moved faster — inches per year — than any other plate, perhaps explaining why geologists consistently characterize the melding of India with Asia as a "collision." After the collision and for the next 50 million years the two continental plates partook in a geologic rodeo, pushing, grinding, buckling, and eventually forcing upward the greatest collection of mountains the earth has ever known. Awestruck explorers proclaimed this landscape of high peaks the "roof of the world" or the "third pole." Seven great ramparts that intertwine twelve central Asian countries include all fourteen of the earth's 26,000+-foot peaks and the vast Tibetan Plateau, with an average elevation of 14,500 feet and a vital watershed to one-fifth of the world's population.

The subcontinent came to Asia a virtual Noah's Ark of wildlife, including a unique assortment of animals that evolved as the mountains grew, adapting to a frosty band of life between permanent ice and tree line. With tens of millions of years to adapt, this snowy Eden evolved predator and prey highly specialized for life in high places. Wild yak, kiang or wild ass, and the Tibetan antelope flourished on the high plains of the Tibetan Plateau. In the rugged high mountains, an assortment of wild sheep and goats found sufficient forage to thrive on south-facing slopes, migrating up and down with the seasons. To keep these herding species in check, nature provided a coursing predator, the wolf, and a stalking predator, the snow leopard. Eventually, in only the last few thousand years, human beings—the ultimate predators—would invade these high reaches. They evolved with a hearty skill for survival and clever ingenuity for eking out a living in high, high places where every blade of grass struggles for life. Until the last few hundred years, life there was difficult but harmonious between human and animal denizens.

Ecologically, the snow leopard ranges throughout more than 1.2 million square miles of high plateau and rugged mountains, an area roughly the size of the western United States. Politically, these ranges fall within twelve countries: Uzbekistan, Tajikistan, Russia, Pakistan, Nepal, Mongolia, Kyrgyz Republic, Kazakhstan, India, China, Bhutan, and Afghanistan. China alone contains about 60 percent of the snow leopard's suitable range. Few species contend with such a varied physical and political landscape. In the halls of government the species is revered, protected (at least on paper), and used to symbolize cross-border conservation unity. On the ground, the snow leopard continues to lose habitat as new roads and pastoral expansion bring more and more humans into its once peaceful world. With more than 600 snow leopards in zoos, no more are being taken from the wild.

Though defenseless against political influences, the snow leopard is extremely well adapted for living in higher altitudes, typically between 11,500 and 23,000 feet above sea level. Its big chest and large nasal cavity help accommodate maximum oxygen intake. Long legs, snowshoe-like paws, and a long tail help this big cat cruise deep snow and steep, rugged terrain. Its exceptional tail helps with balance when the animal is bolting up to thirty feet across boulders, and it provides warmth when curled around the body. Weighing in at 60 to 120 pounds, snow leopards are formidable-sized cats and, like most cat species, are efficient killers. Unlike lions and tigers, snow leopards have never been known to harm humans. Some experts speculate that their fear of humans is a result of the relatively short, limited exposure snow leopards have had to upright walkers. Even in remote mountain villages, residents may never see a snow leopard in their lifetimes. Unfortunately, snow leopards occasionally stray from their normal diet of wild sheep and goats, taking domestic stock. In an enclosed stock pen filled with sheep or goats, a single snow leopard can kill over 100 animals in one night—a devastating financial loss for the unlucky family. Crepuscular, they prefer hunting in late evening and early morning. Their smoky-gray fur with black spots and dark rosettes matches their surroundings, creating the perfect cloak for the ghost of the mountain to play tricks on the inferior human eye.

These cool cats are mostly loners, coming together only for mating, which may take just a week. Territories are marked heavily to avoid conflict and define boundaries: using their hind feet, snow leopards scratch shallow indentations called scrapes along travel corridors, often leaving scat or urinating on the scrape. They also cheek-rub and spray scent on overhanging rocks to forewarn other cats of territorial boundaries. The mating season is timed to coincide with prey abundance: mating occurs in January through March, and gestation lasts about 100 days, at which time two to three cubs are born in a secluded cave or crevice. The peak birthing period is May or June, which coincides with the greater abundance of newborn sheep and goats. Cubs are fully reliant on the mother as provider and teacher for eighteen to twenty-two months.

The snow leopard's world is seasonal, and like all predators they must follow their prey. Spring and summer is the time of new cubs, a time of abundant prey that migrates to higher-elevation pastures. In the fall, prey moves lower down the valleys. For females with cubs, especially last year's cubs now about a year-and-a-half old and nearly the size of adults, there is greater demand for hunting. Winter is the difficult time, a frozen landscape of white and gray. Winter coats grow up to 4.5 inches of new hair to hold in warmth. Prey are lower and in tight herds, but they are more wary and deep snow makes hunting more difficult. This is also the time of greatest conflict with humans, especially if natural prey is gone or scarce. On rare occasions, hunger or simply a unique opportunity causes snow leopards to kill domestic animals. Local villagers, also surviving marginally, are compelled to kill the night stalker.

Though protected under the Convention on International Trade in Endangered Species and the Endangered Species Act, snow leopards continue to fall prey to deliberate poaching for bones and skin, loss of habitat, and lack of adequate parks and protected areas. Luckily, a growing number of organizations have stepped up efforts to reduce human conflict with local villagers and have brought incentive programs for active community-level conservation. Although estimates of the overall total number of snow leopards range from 4,500 to 7,500, the real threats to the species are at the population level, where competition is keenest between cats and humans. In addition, the snow leopard faces a new threat: climate change. Given its narrow, fragile life zone, it stands to reason that climate change, especially global warming, will accelerate the species toward local extinction. Just as polar bears are affected by the latitudinal, *pole-ward* warming of the Arctic, snow leopards are susceptible to the altitudinal, *upward* warming of higher elevations.

As the high mountains warm, the snow leopard and its prey will try to adapt, but suitable habitat is finite—there is no place beyond the mountaintops. Warming in Asia's high mountains will cause glaciers to retreat and alter rainfall patterns; as growing seasons lengthen, grassland will migrate upward. These conditions let local pastoralists linger higher and longer in mountain pastures, which in turn pushes snow leopards and their prey into higher, less productive, more precipitous mountain terrain. In many locations these changes decrease historic range, forcing snow leopards into unsuitable habitat and shrinking their already limited range. These conditions also set the stage for conspecific competition with cats of traditionally lower elevations, such as the clouded leopard and tiger. Local extinctions are a certainty. Many of today's leading experts on snow leopards believe these extinctions are already occurring.

The fate of the snow leopard rests in the hands of the local people who share their world. They are not alone, however, in the struggle to coexist with the snow leopard. They are helped by a cadre of extraordinary people driven to protect this rare cat and its fragile world. In the stories that follow, these people speak on behalf of the snow leopard. Read slowly and linger for a while above the clouds where a rare cat lives.

G E O R G E   B .   S C H A L L E R

ON MEETING A SNOW LEOPARD

PAKISTAN—*A renowned biologist vividly describes his first encounter with a snow leopard and the lofty world it inhabits.*

Whenever I walk through the Bronx Zoo, I like to halt in front of the snow leopards. Their luxuriant smoke-gray coats sprinkled with black rosettes convey an image of snowy wastes, and their pale, frosty eyes remind me of immense solitudes. For a moment the city vanishes and I am back in the Hindu Kush, the home of these magnificent cats.

The December cold gripped the valley as soon as the feeble sun disappeared behind the ridge. The slopes and peaks above an altitude of 11,000 feet were snow-covered, and a bank of clouds along the distant summits suggested that soon so would be the valleys. I hurried down the trail along the edge of a boulder-strewn stream until the valley widened. There I stopped and with my binoculars scanned the steep slope ahead, moving upward past the scree and outcrops, past scattered oak trees and stands of pine, to a cliff over a thousand feet above me. A female snow leopard lay on the crest of a spur, her chin resting on a forepaw, her pelage blending into the rocks so well that she seemed almost a part of them. Several jungle crows sat in a nearby tree, and a Himalayan griffon vulture wheeled overhead, intent, I knew, on the carcass of a domestic goat the leopard was guarding.

I angled up the slope toward her, moving slowly and halting at intervals, seemingly oblivious to her presence. She flattened into the rocks and watched my approach. Once she sat up, her creamy white chest a bright spot among the somber cliffs, then snaked backward off her vantage point to become a fleeting shadow that molded itself to the contours of the boulders. She retreated uphill, crossing open terrain only when a tree or outcrop shielded her from my view. From another rock she peered at me, only the top of her head visible, but a few minutes later she stalked back to her original perch and casually reclined there. I was grateful for her curiosity and boldness, for she was so adept at hiding that I would not have seen much of her without her consent. I halted 150 feet away and in the fading light unrolled my sleeping bag along a ledge in full view of her. Lying in the warmth of my bag, I could observe her feeding at the kill until darkness engulfed us. And then there was only the wind moaning among the boulders and the occasional grating of tooth on bone as the leopard continued her meal.

That night it snowed, heavy moist flakes that soaked through my bedding. I huddled on the ledge, sleeping intermittently, until the rocks once again emerged from the darkness. Over four inches of snow had fallen. As I rolled up my sodden belongings, I envied the snow leopard, which sat protected and dry in the shelter of an overhang. I descended the slope through clouds and falling snow, heading toward the mud-walled hut that was my base camp in the valley. Though I was tired and chilled, the mere thought of having spent the night near a snow leopard filled me with elation.

With the support of the New York Zoological Society and the National Geographic Society, Zahid Beg Mirza of Punjab University and I had come to Chitral in West Pakistan to make a month-long wildlife survey in the Chitral Gol reserve. This reserve, comprising about thirty square miles of rugged mountains with peaks rising to an altitude of 17,500 feet, has for many years belonged to the royal family of Chitral. Now His Highness Saif-ul-Maluke hopes to convert the area from a hunting reserve into a private sanctuary where visitors might observe the wildlife. Of particular interest to us were the Kashmir markhor goats, one of seven subspecies of *Capra falconeri*.

The markhor spend May to October at timberline and above, but they winter in the valleys where there is less snow and more food. In the Chitral Gol, evergreen oak trees provide the markhor with their main winter forage. It was startling to see these goats clamber with amazing agility among the branches of an oak tree, as high as twenty feet aboveground, as they searched for tender twigs and leaves. Most of the herds we saw were small, ranging from two to eighteen individuals, and usually consisted of several females — many of them accompanied by one or two kids, a yearling or two, and often some young males. Each herd tended to confine its movements to a particular locality.

On the other hand, the adult males, easily recognizable by their long, spiraling horns and flowing white neck ruff, roamed widely, either alone or in small groups. In late November and early December some adult males joined the females in the herds, the first sign of the rut that was to reach its peak in late December. Only one large adult male accompanied a herd during the rut, a good indication that at that time relations between rivals were strained. Our census showed that about 100 to 125 markhor wintered in the reserve. The population was healthy and breeding was good. An average of 1.3 kids accompanied each adult female and 16.5 percent of the population consisted of yearlings. If poaching could be fully controlled and the range less heavily used by domestic stock, the Chitral Gol might some day become the most important refuge for this increasingly rare goat.

One day, shortly after our arrival, we found old snow leopard tracks crossing a snowdrift at 11,000 feet, and I became determined to meet one of these cats. Snow leopards live in the mountains of central Asia, usually occurring above an altitude of 5,000 feet, although in some areas, such as the Pzhungarian Ala-Tau of the USSR, they are found as low as 3,000 feet. Their range extends from the Hindu Kush in Afghanistan eastward along the Himalayas and across Tibet to the Szechwan Province of China and northeast-ward along the Pamir, Tien Shan, and Altai ranges to the Sayan Mountains that straddle the border between Mongolia and Russia near Lake Baykal.

Because of its remote habitat, coupled with its shy nature and rarity, the snow leopard remains the least known of the great cats. Most published accounts say little more than that they migrate seasonally up and down the mountains with the herds of wild sheep and goats that constitute their principal prey. Only occasionally do such accounts contain an interesting bit of information. In the Khirgiz Ala-Tau, for instance, snow leopards are said to rest in nests built by black vultures in low juniper trees, and a Russian biologist watched two snow leopards play, rearing up on their hind legs and exchanging blows before "arching their backs at one another" and parting. Hari Dang, an Indian mountaineer, has seen snow leopards repeatedly, and his article "The Snow Leopard and Its Prey," published in the October 1967 issue of the journal *Cheetal*, represents the best attempt so far to gather information about this elusive cat.

For a week I searched for snow leopards, following tracks until they disappeared among the crags. A snow leopard in a zoo may mark its cage by rubbing its face sinuously against a log, scraping the floor alternately with its hind paws, and then turning — its tail raised and quivering — and squirting a mixture of scent and urine. At other times, it may scrape and then defecate at the site. Now, in the wild, I found similar signs. Occasionally a pungent odor on a tree trunk or rock told me where a snow leopard had left its "calling card," and scrapes, with or without feces, also advertised its presence. The feces revealed what the animals had eaten. I examined sixteen droppings; of these, five contained markhor hair, eight the remains of domestic sheep and goats, two solely a large-leafed herb, and one just earth.

Judging by tracks, a female with a cub and a small lone animal, probably a sub-adult, frequented the Chitral Gol during our visit, but other snow leopards no doubt also roamed through the area at times. The tracks showed that snow leopards, like most cats, were essentially solitary except, of course, when a female had cubs. Hari

Dang saw snow leopards sixteen times, of which twelve sightings were of animals alone and the rest of pairs. But whether the pairs consisted of a male and a female, a large cub with its mother, or members of the same sex was not specified. Nothing is known about the social system of snow leopards, and I wonder if adults are truly unsociable, like the African leopard, or if they may meet, tarry awhile together, and perhaps share a kill before parting again, as is the case among tigers.

I soon realized that my chances of meeting a snow leopard were slim. The cats were rare, and they traveled far each day in search of food. The large herds of domestic sheep and goats that forage on the alpine meadows in summer had been taken to the villages. Marmots were hibernating. All that remained were scattered herds of markhor and various small animals, such as black-naped hare and chukar partridge, which could provide a snack at most for a predator that may weigh as much as 100 pounds and reach a length of six-and-a-half feet.

The lack of food in winter may force snow leopards into the cultivated valleys, where they lurk around villages with the hope of capturing an unwary dog or other domestic animal. Often they are rewarded with a bullet instead. The demand for spotted furs by the fashion industry has also provided an incentive for killing the cats. Although both India and Pakistan prohibit the commercial export of snow leopards, any number of skins can be bought in local markets for about $150 apiece and smuggled without trouble out of these countries in personal luggage. The International Fur Trade Federation has agreed to impose a total ban on trade in snow leopard skins among its members, a step that will hopefully reduce the demand for this fur.

Having obtained some idea of the favored routes of the snow leopards in the Chitral Gol, I staked out a domestic goat as bait at five different locations. Daily for two weeks I checked each goat, feeding and watering it when necessary, yet the cats eluded me. One night a snow leopard passed within 150 feet of a goat, apparently without seeing it, for the tracks continued without deviation or break in stride.

I had almost given up hope of a meeting when early one morning a sanctuary guard hurried toward me, pointing with his stick at the sky and grinning broadly. Circling high over a ridge near one of the goats were several vultures. A kill had been made. And then through my scope I saw the snow leopard at rest on a promontory. Beside her was a tiny cub, a black and white puff of fur about four months old. In captivity the usual litter consists of two cubs, but litters vary from one to four young. Later I was told by the sanctuary staff that this female had been seen with two cubs the previous month.

According to the literature, cubs are usually born in April and May. Assuming a gestation period of 98 to 103 days, as determined in zoos, this cub had been conceived at that time and been born in August. Soon afterward the cub retreated into a cleft among the rocks and remained out of sight all day while its mother continued to guard the kill. Once a bold crow landed near the carcass and the female rushed at the bird, her movements remarkably smooth in spite of her stocky, powerful build. Afterward she reclined again, dozing or gazing over her domain. At dusk the cub rejoined its mother, greeting her in typical cat fashion by rubbing its cheek against hers. They then fed. On subsequent days they followed the same routine, with the result that I seldom was able to observe the cub.

Daily for a week I watched the snow leopards, sometimes concealed on the opposite side of the valley, at other times near them. I moved a little closer each day until the female permitted me to approach to within 120 feet. Since she spent hour after hour at rest and the cub remained hidden, my behavioral observations were rather limited in scope.

At times I was able to watch a herd of markhor on a distant slope. The rut was now reaching its peak. If there was a female in heat, a large male might follow her closely, holding himself very erect until suddenly he lowered his neck and stretched his muzzle forward while his tongue flicked in and out of his mouth. With a jerk he twisted his head sideways, at the same time kicking a foreleg into the air. To this display the female markhor would often respond by walking hurriedly away. The male followed, which in turn caused her to move faster, until both rushed along the slope and through the trees.

At other times there were birds to observe. Two bearded vultures might be tumbling over and over in a display of aerial exuberance, their hawk-like screams the only sounds among these snow-flecked crags, or I might tally the bird species that passed by me—alpine chough, nutcracker, black-throated jay, pied woodpecker, and others.

After the snow leopards had eaten one goat, I gave them another and then a third. The female killed the last one late in the afternoon, as I watched. She advanced slowly down the slope, body pressed to the ground, carefully placing each paw until she reached a boulder above the goat. There she hesitated briefly, then leaped to the ground. Whirling around, the startled goat faced her with lowered horns. Surprised, she reared back and swiped once ineffectually with a paw. When the goat turned to flee, she lunged in and with a snap clamped her teeth on its throat. At the same time she grabbed the goat's shoulders with her massive paws. Slowly it sank to its knees, and, when she tapped it lightly with a paw, it toppled on its side. Crouching or sitting, she held its throat until, after eight minutes, all movement ceased. Judging by tooth marks on the throat, she had also killed the two previous goats by strangulation.

Hari Dang once watched a snow leopard attack a Himalayan tahr, a type of wild goat: "We were lying behind a boulder watching the thar [sic] climbing leisurely up the scree and the rock overhangs towards the north ridge of Raj Ramba peak, when a flash of white and grey fur dived into the spread out herd and rolled down some hundred feet, all the time hanging on to a young thar ewe." At that point the snow leopard was disturbed by the observer and fled. Dang noted further that "of 17 natural kills seen, 11 were deduced on the basis of the evidence of the tracks to have been made in daytime, generally the early morning and late afternoon." In contrast to my observations, he found that of "34 natural and domestic kills . . . most were neatly killed, either with the neck or the spine broken."

One night the snow leopards departed. I traced their tracks past some outcrops and through a stand of pine before deciding to leave the animals in peace. My meeting with them had been brief, too brief to teach me much of consequence, but on seeing the line of tracks continue upward, I hoped that some day I would return and learn more about the life of these phantoms of the snow.

No one knows how many snow leopards inhabit the mountains of central Asia, but the animal is thought to be rare enough to warrant inclusion in the Red Data Book of the world's threatened species. Though the habitat of the snow leopard seems inaccessible, pastoralists and hunters penetrate the remotest valleys and plateaus, shooting the cats and depriving them of their natural prey. Only large and strictly protected reserves may ultimately help the snow leopard to survive in the wild. Several reserves besides the Chitral Gol contain a few of the cats, among them, for example, the Nanda Devi and Dachigam Sanctuaries in India and the Aksu-Dzhabagly Sanctuary in the USSR, but those in South Asia receive at best only the most cursory protection. Zoos are assuming increasing importance as repositories of breeding stock of threatened species. When in 1903 the Bronx Zoo received its first snow leopards, only two others were on exhibition elsewhere, in London and Berlin. By 1970 a total of ninety-six snow leopards resided in forty-two zoos, according to the *International Zoo Yearbook*. But of these only twenty were bred in captivity, a dismal record. Zoos still draw most of their animals from the wild, principally from the Tien Shan Mountains of Russia, because animals born in captivity seldom live to reproduce.

On seeing a snow leopard in a cage, I can forget the bars and remember when we met on a desolate slope in a world of swirling snow. May others, too, find such private visions until the end of time.

JOSEPH L. FOX

FACE-TO-FACE WITH SHAN

INDIA—After much searching, a professor from a Norway university finds himself face-to-face with a snow leopard.

She had been on a kill for the past two days. Though partially obscured by thick brush, we could see her feeding. On the dawning of the third day, crawling from my bitterly cold tent, I spotted her emerging from the brush. She climbed steadily up the sparsely vegetated walls of the gorge surrounding our camp. On an impulse, I grabbed my camera and decided to follow, knowing full well that pursuing a snow leopard on foot up a steep ridge was not likely to result in anything but exhaustion on my part. She went out of view about 500 yards ahead of me, straight up rocky terrain. Climbing as fast as I could in the lean air of 11,000 feet, I began to despair that this would be my last image of this magnificent cat.

Eager for another glimpse, I kept climbing in hopes that she would still be in sight. Just as I moved around the sharp ridgeline at a slight easing of the steep pitch, there she was, immediately in front of me, lying on a rocky ledge—not more than twenty yards away. Face-to-face, we stared at each other, neither moving as time slowed for what seemed like minutes but may have been only seconds. I was stunned to be so close, feeling no fear, just frozen in the presence of this apparition, this mystical cat I had spent months searching for. She lay there calmly on the rock, staring back with dark wary eyes, showing no sign of alarm. Motionless but still breathing heavily from the steep climb, my mind raked in the vision in front of me, my spirit buoyed by the gift of just being there. Finally, breathing more easily and with steadying hands, I raised my camera slowly and took a photo. She then rose gracefully and walked leisurely farther up the steep ridgeline; her long tail swept the air as she skirted a rocky promontory. I followed, desperate to stretch this magical, once-in-a-lifetime moment. She granted one more glimpse, one more fleeting picture as her luxuriant gray and off-white fur suddenly vanished into a wall of rock.

This unforgettable encounter happened in 1985 in Ladakh, India, a land sometimes called "Little Tibet" for its ethnic and scenic similarity to neighboring Tibet. It was near a small seasonal livestock-herder camp high up in the Zanskar Mountains in the secluded Markha Valley, about thirty miles south of Ladakh's main town, Leh. Word of a stock-raiding snow leopard had come down the valley to me and my field companion, Raghu Chundawat. We hurried up-valley and arrived at the herder camp about midday. It consisted of a few tightly arranged stone houses, tent-site enclosures, and livestock corrals that provided primitive shelter during spring and autumn. It was early March, and the camp was inhabited only by two young girls who looked to be about ten years old. They occupied one of the tiny houses and daily herded their families' several hundred goats and a few sheep to graze in the valley bottom and on nearby slopes.

On the day we arrived, their livestock spooked easily, still wary as a result of a raiding snow leopard two days earlier. The young girls were vigilant as well. We set up camp a little down-valley from their stone house, at the edge of dense thickets of buckthorn and willow in the valley bottom. Within hours of our arrival, Raghu heard the girls yelling "shan, shan," the Ladakhi name for snow leopard. The stealthy shan had just killed several goats in the thick brush right at the edge of camp, not more than thirty yards from our tents. The young shepherdesses raced to protect their animals, frantic in their efforts to gather in the remaining herd and at the same time create a disturbance to drive the leopard away. Young but fearless, they went into thickets, throwing rocks and willow sticks at the snow leopard, trying to drive it away so they could retrieve their dead animals. Such fearlessness by the youngsters testifies to the hearty stock of these mountain people and the general lack of serious danger in approaching snow leopards. One would never do this with a common leopard. But it highlighted for me the vulnerability of snow leopards, which are often cornered in such circumstances and stoned to death by local villagers. Conversely, here was the very reason I was in these mountains, this magnificent and almost mythical snow leopard, causing havoc and despair for two young girls responsible for their families' precious livestock. I was looking for signs of this endangered species, with the goal of initiating conservation efforts. The girls found it unfathomable that we wanted to stay nearby and observe the shan as it consumed one of their goats. We purchased the last goat kill before the girls retrieved it, leaving it for the snow leopard so we could observe its behavior on the kill. Despite explanations of our efforts, we could not bring the girls to understand our fascination with this predator. Their reaction was perfectly understandable: the snow leopard took sheep and goats, the families' sole livelihood. Reconciling these different views of the same animal underscores the dilemma of conserving this endangered cat. For two days we watched as the snow leopard slowly consumed the dead goat. The young girls went about herding, grudgingly accepting the snow leopard in their midst while guiding their animals elsewhere for grazing and marveling at our fascination with the shan.

For many years after this amazing encounter I directed my energies to educational and research activities in Ladakh, exposing others to the beauty of this mythical place and adding kindred spirits to the ranks of conservation supporters. I had the good fortune to establish a university-based teaching career that included snow leopard research. My graduate students from Nepal, Mongolia, and the Tibetan areas of China, as well as the Ladakh region of

India, have spent countless hours in unique mountain classrooms throughout central Asia. Ladakh has become one of the best-known areas for snow leopards in the world, attracting thousands of tourists, intense conservation efforts, and world-class documentary filmmakers and photographers. Such attention, along with a better scientific understanding of snow leopards, has altered the human–snow leopard dynamic in recent years. Locals have learned that visitors from other parts of India and around the world are willing to pay for the privilege of visiting snow leopard country.

Along with colleagues in India, we arranged for visitors to help fund and carry out fieldwork excursions, first through the School for Field Studies and later through Earthwatch. Eventually, other conservation organizations entered the picture and established programs in this area. Such notoriety and the accompanying benefits to locals have helped to dissipate animosity toward the leopard's occasional stock raiding. Today, local herders, horsemen, farmers, shop owners, home-stay entrepreneurs, and nature guides value "shan," favoring conservation over extermination. But as livelihoods improve and personal desires change, human interaction with the snow leopard takes on more complicated nuances, calling repeatedly for new approaches to effective conservation.

Now, more than twenty-five years after the encounter with which I opened these reflections, I still have a vivid picture in my mind of that early-morning climb and reflect on how those months in northern India, searching for a snow leopard, contributed to a pattern that shaped my life and career. By luck or perhaps karma, I was able to carve out a working life that allowed me to return many times to the land of the snow leopard. A Tibetan refugee colleague from my early Peace Corps days in Nepal, who was with me the first time I encountered snow leopard tracks on a snowy Himalayan ridge top, will soon visit me at my new home in the Colorado Rockies. I look forward to showing him the special places I know and love here. Maybe we will see cougar tracks in the snow. I'm hopeful that the snow leopard will continue to live wild and free, leaving tracks for us to know of its presence for endless generations.

JAN E. JANECKA

TRACKS OF MY SOUL

MONGOLIA—*A geneticist follows the tracks of his inner compass to snow leopard country.*

One of my earliest memories, from when I was maybe three or four years old, is of my father, Lubomir, singing a lullaby he had written for me. At that time we lived in former Communist Czechoslovakia, far from the mountains of central Asia, many worlds away from snow leopards. As political refugees, my family was forced to immigrate to the United States, where I would later start my career as a scientist. The words of my father's song have faded, but I can clearly remember the images that drifted through my mind in that dreamy time just before sleep. The song was about the Great Steppe of Asia, desolate, remote, calling to me. I would fall into my dreams immersed in an endless world of adventure, feeling the cold bite of the crisp dry air passing over the mountains, the piercing howl of wolves off in the distance. These images touched me, leaving tracks in my soul that beckoned me to follow.

Twenty-five years later, as I stood next to a simple stupa over-looking the rugged mountains of Ladakh, thoughts of my child-hood surfaced as I contrasted my surrounds with the images of youthful dreams. It was my first time in this ruggedly beautiful land, yet standing there, tiny among the mighty peaks of the Himalayas, I felt as though I had come home. A loving melody of adventure had brought me to a strange land in search of the snow leopard, central Asia's most mythical cat. It was Christmas. Alone in a chilly hotel room in Leh, missing my family but filled with eagerness for the adventure ahead, a warmth fell over me as I knew for certain that I had reached this moment by following tracks laid down in my soul long ago.

Later, these tracks would guide me to Mongolia, where the beauty and wonder of the Gobi Desert overwhelmed my senses and drew me even closer to the snow leopard. These elusive cats are very difficult to see and count, so my colleagues and I devised a new censusing method called "noninvasive genetics," which uses genetic markers from feces—an approach used since the 1990s for carnivores such as wolves and bears. We hope to prove this technique is a feasible alternative to expensive and difficult live animal studies.

Our plan was to hike into snow leopard habitat and systematically collect scats (feces) for analysis later in our laboratory. From DNA in the scat we can determine the species and sex and mark it as distinguishable from others. This is the same technique as DNA fingerprinting used in forensics to solve crimes. Using this approach, we can locate where snow leopards occur and estimate how many are in a specific area with greater certainty than traditional sign surveys provide.

While working in Mongolia I developed a rapport with Bariushaa Munkhtsog, a Mongolian biologist with over fifteen years of field experience studying snow leopards. In the field, we lived alongside local people and developed a close bond. Even though we were from different cultures with completely different backgrounds, a love for wildlife brought us together, leading to a natural camaraderie. The success of our first scat-collecting expedition led us to prepare a more ambitious project proposal to estimate the population size and distribution of snow leopards throughout Mongolia, including levels of landscape connectivity. During the 2007 Christmas season, while visiting my parents, I received some of the most exciting news of my life: the National Geographic Society had funded our project.

At times I enjoy lab work, writing manuscripts, and hanging out with my Texas A&M friends. But for me, lab work eventually becomes drudgery, and everyday life gets monotonous. It stands in stark contrast to my times in Ladakh or the Gobi, where there is something new each day and everything holds mystery. That is what I love most about being in the field—the unexpected. An unpredictable life is an adventurous life. I missed that adventure and longed to return to the field.

Excited to be back in Mongolia, Munkhtsog, Ganaa (our field assistant), and I flew from Ulaanbaatar to Dalanzadgad, 335 miles to the south. We met with the Gurvan Saikhan National Park administration staff that manages our study area. Gurvan Saikhan means "Three Beauties," a natural jewel of the Gobi Desert named for three mountain ranges in the park: Western Beauty, Middle Beauty, and Eastern Beauty. The park director gave us the go-ahead and signed a contract with Munkhtsog, who was representing the Mongolian Academy of Sciences. The park director later came to our hotel for an informal meeting. He was very friendly and had a good sense of humor. Although I had to speak through Munkhtsog's translation, I was grateful for his gesture of friendship. The next day we picked up two rangers who would be working with us. Our team now complete, we stocked up on supplies and drove to Eastern Beauty, only about 12.5 miles but a two-hour drive because of bad roads.

We had a great team. I was very happy that Lagwa was again part of our team. As on my last trip he was the driver/assistant/mechanic/cook/hardworking jack-of-all-trades. He did not speak much English, but despite the language barrier he laughed easily, and we became good friends. He even helped me learn some Mongolian. Ganaa, our field assistant and the youngest among us, had worked for Munkhtsog on the Pallas cat and other surveys. He also had a good sense of humor, worked very hard, never complained, was sharp, and knew some broken English. The two rangers, Erdenebileg and Battsog, were different characters. Their lean bodies and tanned, weathered faces reflected a life spent in the mountains. They had grown up in the area and worked in the park for over ten years, so they were essential for our success. When I first met Erdenebileg, he looked stern and serious, but I soon realized that he was very generous and good-natured. Battsog possessed a friendly disposition accented by constant but pleasant banter. Munkhtsog's character is well suited to life in the field. Dedicated to research and conservation, he works hard but also enjoys socializing, playing cards, joking, and laughing — a common, endearing Mongolian trait. We had become fast friends during our first survey. I was happy to be working with him again. It was a great team, with everyone dependable and trustworthy yet also a lot of fun, which broke up the hard and at times repetitive work.

The first few days of the survey pushed the limits of my body. College Station, Texas, had no hills. I had run to prepare for this trip, but running isn't quite the same as hiking up mountains. On the first transect, with Battsog and Ganaa in the lead heading up a steep ridgeline, I began to doubt if I was going to make it. My legs felt like wood; at times they exploded with pain, but miraculously I made it to the top. Split into two teams, we typically surveyed one to three miles of game trails or ridgelines, collecting ten to twenty scats in about four hours. Our first scrape, a good omen for the start of the survey, brought great excitement. We also noted other signs of snow leopard, such as tracks and scent spray on rocks.

When we found scat, Battsog and I would break a small piece using two rocks so as not to contaminate it with our DNA. The sample would go into a small glass tube with silica to keep it dry and preserve the DNA. Ganaa would record the Global Positioning System (GPS) location and the number of scrapes nearby. Noninvasive genetic surveys are somewhat like an Easter egg hunt, except you can't eat the eggs. When I was a PhD student, a friend joked that I would make a career out of going around the world collecting crap. He was quite the fortune teller.

After the first transect, we returned to the van, had lunch, and drove about three miles to survey one more area. There we spotted ibex, pika, and ground squirrels—more abundant wildlife than on our previous trip. After finishing our collection for that day, we visited a ger, had dinner, and drank vodka. It is Mongolian tradition that all gers are always open for visitors. Our host jokingly exclaimed, "There is so much gold in the Beauties, I should have gold teeth by now." Locals searching for gold illegally constituted a big problem in the park. We joked in return that if I had brought a metal detector, we would no longer need grant money. Even though the rangers occasionally catch the prospectors, the area is too large to monitor effectively. The prospectors find enough gold to keep digging despite the risk, making it a very difficult problem to solve.

Munkhtsog said that a politician had proposed opening the Three Beauties to gold mining, but the idea was generally unpopular and would likely not pass. I envisioned developing countries as always exploiting minerals and other resources at the expense of wildlife, yet here Mongolians opposed a bill because it would negatively affect a protected wilderness.

After dinner, my sore legs started to recover. The team members played cards, a regular evening event. I tried to pick up the rules but fell asleep confused. The next day we surveyed a site about nine miles from the one the day before. As we drove on the dirt road, pika and ground squirrels scampered on the hillsides and a beautiful red fox appeared, its fur reflecting the morning sun. It wasn't red but rather grayish-white. According to Munkhtsog the foxes molt in the winter, similar to Arctic foxes. A wolf watched us and the fox cautiously from a distant mountainside.

It always surprises me to find so many animals and so much snow leopard sign in these desolate mountains, a landscape of mostly rock and gravelly dirt. A cold place where your lips dry and crack, the sun burns your face, and your legs ache. Yet somehow, delicate little plants burst up through the rocky soil. Life finds a way. Ibex, argali, and pika are abundant enough to sustain red foxes, wolves, snow leopards, lynxes, eagles, and other carnivorous creatures that inhabit this rugged world.

The first day was a real struggle. For a few days I was sore and my legs hurt, but I felt good and energetic. As the days passed I became hardened, welcoming the steep terrain. One day we found scat along a trail running up a ridgeline that led to some shallow caves. As soon as we saw the caves, it was clear that they were used by snow leopards. We found fresh and relic scrapes, tracks, and scats, as well as lots of snow leopard hairs sticking on the rocks. In addition to marking territory with scats and scrapes, snow leopards spray scent onto large boulders and rub their faces in a sideways motion, leaving behind whiskers and facial hair—some still containing viable DNA. Our local guides told us that two adults and two to three cubs were using these caves for shelter.

I wondered if they were nearby, watching us from an outcrop. They blend so perfectly with their surroundings that we held little hope of seeing one in the wild. Hopping from boulder to boulder, we looked around and sighted a steep 66-foot cliff face with a larger cave at the top. This cave had reportedly been used by a snow leopard with two kittens the previous spring. Despite my fatigue and burning legs, my excitement was too great; I had to see into the cave. Once inside I rested, absorbing the incredible view. Ruggedly beautiful mountains surrounded by a vast, endless desert, only the remaining snow and blue sky breaking up the brown hues into a symphony of color. I was moved, sitting in a place where a snow leopard had once rested with her cubs. I felt a deep bond.

As an evolutionary biologist, I am fascinated by the way the harsh mountainous conditions shaped snow leopards, enabling them to live in this treeless environment. As they evolved from common ancestors of the tiger, genetic changes adapted them perfectly for life in the most rugged, challenging, and desolate places in the world. They also thrive in a political world as rugged as the physical one, often complex and at times violent. Rational people shy away from such areas, but these kinds of places draw me in. The fewer the people, the harder to reach, the greater the risk, the more excited I get. Difficulty and hardships shape the body and soul just as the anvil and hammer shape the sword. My parents taught my sister, brother, and me to face adversity and hold onto our faith during hard times. For me, the snow leopard epitomizes the strength to not only survive but to thrive under challenging circumstances. They are awe-inspiring creatures.

On the way back from the snow leopard cave, we visited Battsog's family. He is one of ten siblings, a family size that isn't unusual for Mongolians. In the winter, most of the family lives together in the traditional Mongolian ger. Somewhat magical, the ger's unassuming outer canvas layer fit well with the bleak mountain landscape of the Gobi. But inside the ger was vibrant, alive with color. Colorfully painted crossbeams on the roof and walls framed a lining of Afghan rugs woven into various lively designs of horses, mountains, and ibex. The warmth from the stove was welcoming, and on one side stood a small bookshelf, with family pictures, books, and knick-knacks that must all have a story. The colorful and lively inside of a ger stands in contrast to the drab landscape, dominated by tans and grays.

The smiles and laughter of three generations filled Battsog's family ger. Warm greetings from the children, the mom and dad, and grandparents met me. They poured tea and offered cheese curds and small pastries, along with generous toasts of vodka. Joking and laughter echoed through the ger. I was half a world away from Texas, but I felt as though I just had come home.

Back at home, I often find myself recalling the days with warm friendly people, mountains climbed, and new horizons explored beneath the gaze of an unseen rare cat. I miss the people and the rugged world of the snow leopard and long to return. As I ponder the source of this deep longing, my father's lullaby drifts into my mind, a peaceful reminder to heed the tracks of my soul.

HELEN FREEMAN

KASHMIR

INDIA—*On behalf of the snow leopard, a middle-aged woman endures an arduous trek into a mountain paradise and is rewarded in the end with an unexpected gift.*

I read a travel guidebook on India that said it did not matter if the traveler was on the ground or in the air, the visitor's first view of Kashmir would be unforgettable. The Mughal emperors who came here coined a word for the valley: paradise.

As the guidebook said, it was unforgettable, but it was not what I had expected. Instead of relaxing in paradise, I was freezing and scared stiff. Heavy snow was falling and the trail was icy. I kept muttering to myself, "Explain it again, why did I want to do this?" Then, after hours of questioning myself and not getting a satisfactory answer, I turned to pleading: "Please, please, let our destination be around the next bend. I promise to eat bran muffins instead of chocolate." But when darkness fell and we still had not reached our destination, I concentrated on only one thing: survival.

It had all begun innocently enough about a year earlier when I was visiting India's wildlife parks and met Colonel John Wakefield, a former hunter and now an ardent wildlife conservationist. He had been born in India to English parents. Although as a boy he had been sent to school in England, he claimed those years did not count—India was his only home. He had the title of colonel because he had been an officer in the Indian army.

I learned with delight and surprise that he had actually glimpsed a snow leopard in the wild, a rare sight bestowed on only a lucky few. Over the tour's three weeks we discussed what was happening to the species in the high mountains of central Asia, its natural habitat. I told him I had started a nonprofit foundation, the Snow Leopard Trust, to help this endangered species.

Then, before I left to return to the United States, he said he might be able to help set up a special project. A friend of his was in charge of the wildlife department for Jammu and Kashmir (J&K), an area in northern India and the place where he had seen his snow leopard. But it was difficult to get into J&K, and special permits were required. John cautioned me not to do anything regarding that region but rather to wait and let him pursue the matter at his own pace.

I knew very little about J&K, and as soon as I got home I hurried to look it up. Every article emphasized that ever since the English had partitioned India and set up Pakistan in the 1940s, J&K has been what is understatedly called "a conflicted area." Both India and Pakistan claim the entire territory, and wars have been fought over it. Furthermore, endowed with a unique geopolitical status on the Indian subcontinent, J&K has boundaries with Russia, Afghanistan, Pakistan, China, and Tibet. From both the civilian and military points of view, the region is a boiling cauldron.

The border between Pakistan and J&K is dangerous because there are fanatics everywhere. Also, since both countries claim the region as rightfully belonging to them, both have armies right up to the disputed border, and the soldiers shoot at each other fairly often. To make matters worse, the local people have their own very strong opinions on what to do. Basically, it is hard to make any-one happy because everybody wants independence from everyone else.

In my search for information I had found a large map of the area and spread it on the floor. Something caught my eye and I said to my husband, Stan, "This looks good. There is a long, red dotted line across a big portion of the state. It must be a famous trail." Stan eyed it closely and said, "Take another look. It means disputed border territory."

Not good. The chances of doing a snow leopard project there were slim to zero; it would take a small miracle for foreigners to get permission to go there and conduct a study.

Months went by. Then one day, when I was out on the zoo grounds, my secretary contacted me to say that a man from Cashmere was there to see me.

The visitor did not look like anybody from the Cashmere I knew, a quiet little town in eastern Washington where they grow apples. Could he be from Kashmir, India, the place immersed in intrigue, violence, and — I hoped — snow leopards?

The man was dressed in an expensive Savile Row suit, quite handsome, and with regal bearing. He introduced himself as Mir Inayat Ullah, the chief conservator of wildlife for Jammu and Kashmir. He said, "Colonel Wakefield suggested I talk with you." A miracle had happened.

We talked all afternoon about wildlife and mountains. He told me of his dream to have the world know about the magnificent flora and fauna of northern India. I told him about my love for the snow leopard and that the Snow Leopard Trust was now in a position to take on a large project.

Inayat Ullah said he would go back to India and work to get the necessary permits for a snow leopard study. It was obvious that he was proud of the wildlife in his region, and he wanted the rest of the world to appreciate the richness of his land. He said this study was important to him because the snow leopard was the signature species of J&K.

I had no doubt that Inayat would have considerable authority to promote such a project in J&K. But, although he knew the requirements for India, he was more than a little vague on what needed to be done on the US side. He suggested I call someone named David Frugose with US Fish and Wildlife in Washington, DC. He did not have the man's phone number or address, but he said he could locate them when he got back to India.

I couldn't wait. The next day I called Steve Kohl, the only person I knew in Washington, DC, who worked for the US Fish and Wildlife Service. I apologized for asking such a far-out question because I knew there were thousands of people in Fish and Wildlife, but could he possibly know a David Frugose who has connections with India? He said to wait a minute and I heard him yell down the hall, "Hey Dave, are you there? The phone is for you." Without a proper name, office number, or address, the right person had been found. It was a good omen.

The man's name was actually David Ferguson. Without his guidance, skill, and assistance, the snow leopard project in India would never have started or continued.

Dave Ferguson explained that it was highly unusual to have the request come from India for a research project. More often the instigation was from someone on the US side who wanted to go to India to work. As I had surmised, J&K was an especially difficult area in which to get permission for foreigners. But because the initial contact was coming from an official in J&K, we had a better chance. And so the voluminous letters, cables, and phone calls began.

In the end, it was decided that it would be best to have me go over first for a pre-project visit before we actually tried to obtain the necessary signatures for a long-term research study. Inayat Ullah also wanted me to trek in a wildlife sanctuary called Dachigam and to get over a pass and into a high region called Zanskar. He said he wanted me to get a sense of whether it was good snow leopard habitat.

My background is in animal behavior, and I have minimal training in habitat assessment. So I asked a young man who had recently completed his PhD in biology to accompany me. Eric Dinerstein and I had corresponded for several years because he had developed an interest in snow leopards. He had been with the Peace Corps in Nepal, knew Hindi fluently, spoke passable Urdu, and was an enthusiastic naturalist. Eric jumped at the chance. He had a rhino project on the calendar but it would not start for several months, so he was free to join me.

I quickly realized that Eric was brilliant, but I began to wish fervently that he had been endowed with a little more patience. He had spent years studying and now did not want to take any time in dusty, crowded, overly hectic New Delhi going from office to office drinking tea with officials. But then, I told myself, who did?

However, it was a chance to put a face to a person and form my own impression of the people we would be working with. Dave Ferguson in DC and the US Embassy in New Delhi arranged the introductions. Even if all the talk over tea was in generalities, I thought it would help move the forthcoming multiyear research study through the intricate cogs of the vast Indian bureaucracy. I was afraid someone might get the impression they had been left out of the loop and possibly tie up the project for months. However, it was one cup of lukewarm office tea too many for Eric, and relations between us became strained.

Finally, though, that part was finished, and we flew north to Srinigar. With its sumptuous gardens and location on fabled Lake Dal, the city was once the center of the Moghul Empire. It was also the place where the British Raj, when the sun never set on their empire and they ruled all over the globe, went to escape the oppressive heat of Delhi.

The flight took several hours. Looking out the plane window at the snow-covered peaks, I could not believe what I was seeing. So many high summits, close together and everywhere. I had thought the mountains near Seattle were impressive but these giants went on forever. It seemed as though I was viewing this and my whole trip in a dream and that I was not actually there.

The arrival in Srinigar was an abrupt back-to-earth because the tarmac was ringed with large tanks. Uniformed soldiers with submachine guns at the ready stood on either side of us as we left the plane and walked us into the terminal.

Inside, Inayat Ullah, looking suave and stately, was waiting with a large smile. With him were several younger men, dressed in suits, every hair in place. They all deferred to Inayat.

We went directly to the office for a cup of, you guessed it, tea. But this tea was an elixir of the gods. Inayat, with great ceremony, prepared and served it. To a special Kashmiri blend of tea he added ground almonds, honey, and other magical ingredients. Upon our first sip Eric and I smiled while Inayat looked on expectantly and then beamed. Eric relaxed noticeably. (At this writing Eric is chief scientist and vice president for science for World Wildlife Fund–US and although he does not know it, he owes it all to this restorative cup of tea.)

Inayat had already set up our itinerary. When we had originally started talking about visiting J&K, he had urged me to come during the summer months. That would be the best time, he said, to trek into the mountains. However, he said, if that time was not possible, we should plan to be there no later than September. In October the weather could turn bitterly cold within hours, and the mountain trails would be covered in snow.

But because of the delays in getting permission from so many agencies, it was unfortunately mid-October before we got to Srinigar. So at that first meeting in his office, Inayat Ullah emphasized again that the weather worried him and he was providing me with a sure-footed mountain horse. But I felt like a teenager who could do anything. I asked if I would be required to carry my own pack. He said no, there would be porters for that. So I assured him that if that was the case I could walk and would not need the horse. He said that would be fine but that he was still including the horse. He was right.

Inayat wanted us to become acclimated to ever-higher altitudes, so after a few days in Srinigar he sent us to Dachigam Wildlife Sanctuary. I think he also wanted to show off this jewel of a reserve, one he wanted us to appreciate. Not only was the sanctuary spectacular, but the drive there was beautiful. Nature was decked out in her fall colors, and in the fields women were gathering fruit from the apple trees. (My goodness, I thought, apples— maybe this was more like Washington state's Cashmere than I realized.) But the crocuses that blanketed acres and acres of fields in J&K are not found anywhere in the United States. In Kashmir it is the purple crocus, the plant that produces golden saffron, the most expensive spice in the world.

We were accompanied on our hike by the sanctuary's senior wildlife guard, a small man with a serious look on his face. We found out he was the guide who had accompanied the world-famous biologist George Schaller when he came to Dachigam so I was properly impressed, but, alas, I did not impress this man. When he would point to a spot on the hillside and say something like "Look! There is a purple-throated iridescent giant six-footed beast," I could not find it.

Luckily, we were at the right time of the year for a chance to see the hangul, a subspecies of the red deer, found in the Vale of Kashmir and threatened with extinction. The males were going through rut, and you could hear them bugling. Their distinctive call helped us locate them, and I saw one or two.

But no matter how much our guide tried, he could not help me find the black bear sitting quietly in the deep dark foliage. In Muslim society it is absolutely forbidden for a man to touch a woman who is not a very close relative. In fact, I did not see even husbands and wives touch each other in public. But our guide must have reached a point of extreme frustration because he put his hands over my ears and yanked my head around. I was surprised and he was shocked. It was as if an iron curtain had dropped between us. For the rest of the afternoon he would not even look at me.

When we got back to Srinigar it was time to get ready for our main trek into Zanskar. It was a long drive to the trailhead and, although we had planned to start early in the morning, it was late morning before we got moving. To get to the place where the trek started, we rode in something that in its better days might have been a very old jeep.

I had a seat in the front on a box wedged between the driver and Eric. Three of Inayat's men sat in back. In front of me was the gearshift, and every time the driver shifted, gas fumes poured through a crack on the floorboard. I think I may have gotten a little high because I kept thinking "isn't this grand" and meant it.

At the trailhead, located somewhere on the road between Srinigar and Kargil, our group was waiting: forest guards, porters, pack animals, and, off to the side, a little forlorn horse. He must have known what was ahead for him because we soon found that the trail went only one way, and that direction was up. The horse was starting to look better to me.

Happy to be in the field at last, Eric walked steadfastly in the lead accompanied by one of Inayat's men and a forest guard. The rest of us were a sorry lot and followed in a haphazard order.

The porters carried wooden boxes, live chickens, packs, and army-issue heavy canvas camping gear. One man with a pack on his back also carried a chaise lounge chair on his head because Inayat thought I might want it for a bed. Another porter, with arms in front and palms turned up, held dozens of eggs in cardboard cartons stacked two feet high. (I figured this meant we were going to eat the poor chickens and not wait for them to lay eggs.) Behind me, led by a quiet villager, was my mountain pony.

At the very back was one of Inayat's men, still wearing his tailored sport coat and holding a transistor radio tight to his ear, lagging so he could listen as long as possible to a cricket match.

Cricket has taken on almost mythical proportions in India and Pakistan, and the match that day was an important one. In this part of Asia a cricket match transcends religion and politics, and emotions run high. Hundreds of millions of people either watch on television or listen on the radio. Each cricket match is like a Super Bowl that goes on for eight or nine hours.

When either a good pitch or a score was made, the fellow with the radio would call it out to the person in front of him, and it would travel down (or I should say up) to the beginning of the line. We belonged in a surrealistic movie by the Italian film director Frederico Fellini.

A few more hours of trekking and we stopped in a little village for tea. Not many foreigners passed that way (in fact, not much of anything passed that way) and seeing a woman, let alone a middle-aged woman, on this route was rare. Everywhere I looked, curious children, parents, and grandparents were staring at me. I wished one of my women friends was here so we could giggle together. I tried to keep smiling, but it felt artificial and must have been a very goofy smile.

A few more hours and we stopped for a short lunch. By now I was having a hard time keeping up. When Eric asked me how I was doing I responded with one of my most memorable denial statements: "Just fine."

At this point the porters decided to strike. The trail was getting steeper, the sky was a dark gray, and it was turning very cold. The porters knew there would be snow and wanted to be paid in advance. I think they wanted to bolt. But Inayat's men held firm and explained in strong terms that there would be no money until the end, and the crisis was averted.

No denying it, the time had come to ride the horse. The saddle, or what I thought was a leather saddle, was covered by a thin blanket. When I got on it felt suspiciously like wood. The reins and bridle were thin, frayed rope. The stirrups, composed of rope and a bit of metal, were so short my knees made an inverted V—most uncomfortable but at that point I would have ridden bareback wearing a tutu.

As everyone feared, it began snowing heavily, and soon everything was white. At times the trail became narrow, only several feet wide, and there was a steep drop-off on the right side. All, including my horse, walked to the inside as much as possible.

The horse was sure and steady and I was relaxed, eyes shut, when my left foot caught on something and I was yanked abruptly up and backward. In walking close to the inside wall the horse had brushed by a stiff tree root that was sticking out, and it had caught the stirrup. We were good and tangled. But the lovely, lovely pony stood still while I worked my foot out of the stirrup and then the stirrup out of the tree root. My knee felt as if it had been pulled out of its socket, but we were still on the top of the trail and not at the bottom of the cliff.

The villager came up and took the reins. From now on he would lead the horse. Although he did not speak English and I did not speak Urdu, he made me feel better immediately. His smile was shy, and his eyes were warm and caring. I knew I was in good hands.

The going became slower for everyone. In addition to the continuing snowfall, it was now much colder and ice was forming everywhere. My whole body was numb and the higher we went, the harder it was for me to breathe: in addition to my lungs feeling stuffed, I had developed sinus congestion in Delhi's polluted atmosphere and my head was pounding. I was not a happy camper. Night dropped and there was no moon.

At one point the trail went over some icy boulders. The horse slipped and I had to get off. One of the guards helped me over the big rocks, the villager helped the horse, and we kept on. This is when I began to ask myself, "Will I get home?"

We spent the night in a maharajah's old hunting lodge. The structure had almost disintegrated, but there were still a few places with walls and a roof. Eric and I shared a room. The chaise lounge was brought in, and I dutifully put my sleeping pad and bag on top of it and crawled in. No good. Not only was there freezing air above me, there was freezing air swirling underneath me. It was like being cocooned in ice. I shoved the lounge chair to one side and got down on the floor. It was still cold but better.

Eric was concerned and asked how I was. I again replied, "Fine." I was not thinking straight and for some reason I thought that if I said out loud how I was actually feeling, I would fall apart, so I talked very little. Instead, I turned all my energy inward. For someone who loves words, it was a silent time.

When we started the next morning it was still snowing and the drifts were deep in some places. I later learned that the forest guard who was breaking trail had come across the footprint of a leopard and shown it to Eric. We were around 10,000 feet at that time, so there was a possibility that it could have been a snow leopard. I would have liked to have seen it, but I was too far back for them to get me. When I learned about it later, I wanted to push Eric off the mountain for not calling me.

We reached a clearing where there was a small hut and we would spend the night. Eric went on to explore an upper region with the forest guards, but I stayed behind. That evening the porters tried to keep warm by building a small fire in the enclosure next to ours, and all night their smoke drifted in. By now my head was pounding, my breathing was shallow, and my chest felt like a large, flat elephant foot was pressing down on it. A deep, racking cough had developed and what little sleep I got was fitful. I learned later that I had pneumonia.

When we started down the next day we used a different trail. I think it was decided to get me down as quickly as possible to help my breathing, and this trail was faster and steeper.

About fifteen minutes into the descent I was looking down at the snow and rocks when, close to the ridge, I spotted a cat track. I couldn't believe it. Eric was too far ahead for me to call, so I stood and stared at it by myself. I thought, well, now he's forgiven and it is his turn to throw me off the mountain.

Yes, it looked like a snow leopard track. The sun had not yet hit that part of the trail and the pugmark was crisp. It was the same as the snow leopard tracks I had seen so often at the zoo.

This was a complete surprise and a bonus beyond belief. I never expected to cross paths with a wild snow leopard. My first reaction was, cannot be; absolutely cannot be. But then I thought, well, the altitude is high enough. A common leopard would not be up this high, but certainly a snow leopard could wander through here. The chances may be slim but the possibility is real. That was enough for me.

It has been about twenty years since that first trip to Kashmir, and although I have returned to Asia many times, there has been no other trip like it. The contrasting emotions, the enthusiasm, the fear, the loneliness are still vivid. Though there were times during the trek when I worried whether it was worth the risk, I knew at the same time that it was.

This Kashmiri trip was filled with opportunities and grand adventure. It was reaching for the brass ring and catching it.

YASH VEER BHATNAGAR

FROM RICE FIELDS TO SNOWFIELDS

INDIA—*A young biologist who starts his career in sweltering rice fields shifts to the high Himalayas and becomes captivated by the rare cat that roams free there.*

There was a low rumble from the opposite mountain. We rushed out to see the stream turn into a gray, turbid, frothy mass. The sound grew to a deafening roar; huge boulders began tumbling downward, crushing everything in their path, barely missing a farmer's house—sheer natural force and violence grown from barely a streamlet just a few hours ago. I marveled at this spectacle of nature from my base camp deep inside Pin Valley National Park in northern India's Trans Himalaya, the rain-shadow region of the main Himalaya. Rarely did this region receive such heavy monsoonal precipitation. The raging torrent was frightening but at the same time thrilling to behold. But then the clouds parted and the evening sun emerged, coloring the entire landscape in a golden tinge. I stepped outside, sat on a small earthen bench, and looked about in awe and wonder, sipping hot sweet tea spiced with ginger. One thousand feet above the Parahio River, the Phooma Ridge shimmered green with rain-washed grass, its side slopes a tangled mass of multicolored rocks. In the distance, farther downstream, the river danced wildly at the confluence with the Pin River. Upstream, Kalank Turbo Peak at 19,685 feet glistened white. Behind me a group of ten ibex females and their young nibbled fresh sprouts nonchalantly. "What a life," I thought in contentment.

High on the world about me, my mind drifted to an earlier time in my life, a time not nearly so exhilarating. Just a few years ago I was trudging through slush in a paddy field, loaded down with vials and other assorted equipment needed for my master's research. My days passed setting "quadrats"; counting tillers, egg masses, and caterpillars of rice leaffolder; and collecting caterpillars parasitized by wasps. Later I would rear them in the lab to identify the adult parasites. I shuddered just thinking about the sweltering *terai* of the Himalayan foothills, marshland recently converted to sprawling alluvial rice fields. The fact that the work could be exciting and interesting didn't occur to me at the time. I recalled it as one long suffering. But had I continued my career in agriculture, I might have settled down with a good-paying job— probably selling pesticides in a city—with a proper house and not a leaking work hut.

I glanced about again at the distant snowfields, then spotted Dorje Zangpo and Chhimed Dorje, my able and affable assistants. I felt reassured. Indeed, the slog in the rice fields had ended. By Divine Grace I had reached heaven. I was doing what I liked most— my hobby, my passion, had become my career. Fully aware of the mountains, the crisp cool air, and the sound of the river returning to normal melody, I fell into a deep slumber, visions of my life's journey floating in and out of my consciousness.

Pantnagar Agriculture University was close to the Himalaya, and I could often wangle a short bus ride that would set me wandering the beautiful Kumaon hills, from Kathgodam to Munsiari to Pithoragarh. These excursions moved me, fueling a growing thirst to know these mountains up close. By the time of my second master's degree in wildlife science at the Wildlife Institute of India (WII) it was settled: somehow I would conjoin my future with the Himalaya. But doing what? Most of my colleagues were fascinated by a specific taxa or research question. I was captivated by the high mountains but couldn't decide what to do.

I read Jim Corbett's gripping accounts of tiger hunts and jungle lore set in the Kumaon hills I loved to visit. Spellbinding, but Jim didn't help much with ideas for a career in the mountains. Peter Matthiessen's classic *The Snow Leopard* held my interest when he talked of mountain travel, but the philosophical bits went over my head. The snow leopard remained for me a mythical creature, something out of reach, mystery cat of the big mountains. Then I came across *Stones of Silence,* George Schaller's captivating account of his travels and work in the Himalaya, followed by his seminal scientific treatise *Mountain Monarchs.* The fact that India had wild sheep and goats that survived in extremely cold climes and rugged cliffs was news to me. I understood for the first time the differences between sheep and goats, the interesting description and behavior of other mountain ungulates, how they separate out to avoid competition and predators — including the snow leopard. Schaller had struck the mark.

The possibilities and need for conservation seemed endless. The thrill of science and exploration in remote Himalayan tracts where the last "wildlifer" may have been a British hunter a century ago drew me in. I immediately decided to study the hoofed mountain monarchs. Through my studies, I would do my part to help stave off "stones of silence," Schaller's ominous prediction if the wild creatures disappeared from the great mountains. Besides, Himalayan ungulates are fascinating animals and primary prey of the snow leopard. Little did I know that I would study ibex in these fascinating mountains and that this would one day lead me to a career in snow leopard conservation.

My courses at WII provided great experiences, with extensive and comprehensive field insights. Committed faculty set high standards through their personal passion and knowledge and served as my role models. I first went to Pin Valley National Park with my colleague Nima Manjrekar as part of a WII project to document the ecology of the Asiatic ibex. Years of confusion and struggle had finally sorted out, and my first major life dream had begun to unfold: purposeful excursions into the heart of the Himalaya.

Some officials had labeled Pin Valley National Park "the Land of Ibex and Snow Leopard." I had become familiar with Spiti's landscape, its rivers and streams, through great narratives in books and mountaineering articles by Harish Kapadia and with the local culture from the book *Himalayan Wonderland* by M. S. Gill, a civil servant who came here in the 1960s. None of these books, however, prepared me for the view of the land leeward of the Greater Himalaya. The scene when one emerged from the Sutlej gorge was a sight to behold: stark mountains in hues of white, brown, gray, green, and red, crumpled into huge slabs of rock and snow here, bare soil and pasture there. The air crisp, cool. I could soak in that scenery forever.

The exceptional beauty of the landscape, the thrilling and adventurous life, temperatures that reach minus 40 degrees Fahrenheit, and—most important—an amazing amount of data and information on wildlife made the long winters my favorite season for work in Pin Valley. My wife, Krishna, who spent all her life in the warm peninsular India, joined me in my second year of work, a brave task for someone who didn't know that a place like this existed in India. Her companionship and willing adjustments to the modest living conditions gave my work a new energy. There were challenges too, difficult logistics and a hostile, leaking work hut; but they, too, have become part of our treasured nostalgia.

On a warm July day, Chhimed and I left camp to do vegetation plots in the upper slopes of the nearby stream. The thought of laying countless quadrats and counting plants within them was in no way exciting, even though the task was important. We dragged our feet up the slope and soon came across some coarse green paste on a rock. It looked like rumen content. A little farther ahead we saw a bigger clump and some blood, and we soon found a sheep carcass almost completely devoured. As we approached the kill, the first crow appeared. Near the kill we noticed a very fresh scat and one clear pugmark of a snow leopard. We wondered, "Has the snow leopard just left the site?" It appeared so. The narrow, rugged gorge limited visibility and made for poor tracking. Chhimed scoured all around the area, finally coming upon some spoor going upslope along a rocky crest. We quickly followed the scanty sign. The crest was extremely rocky and the adjacent slope full of loose, gray shale: two steps up, slip down one. Chhimed, however, ran ahead like an ibex while I struggled behind. I tried hard to keep up. The thought of following a snow leopard closely sent shivers of excitement down my spine. Up ahead, Chhimed looked around carefully, finding signs on gravel that we hoped were of the leopard. Forty minutes of hot pursuit left me exhausted. At these elevations everyone must develop an individual pace and move accordingly; moving faster or slower becomes tiring. Chhimed reached a rocky overhang on a knoll and looked around. The steep shale slope completely tired me out, so I decided to go a little to my right on firm ground where I could catch my breath. I worried that I might miss a sighting but just couldn't move ahead. The crest fell sharply a few hundred yards to the stream, a place we named Concave Rock, a mass of cliff that appears concave and is often used by ibex.

I had given up on the possibility of a sighting and satisfied myself with the thought that we had at least gotten close to a snow leopard. Chhimed also looked frustrated. From where he stood, he had a clear view of the entire slope above and the concave rock below. There was no sign of the leopard. But then it happened. I heard a few rocks tumbling and suddenly, only a few feet from me, a very surprised snow leopard screeched to a halt just in time to avoid bumping into me. It happened quickly, but my mind slows the scene each time I think of it: startled round eyes, screeching forelegs, tail drawn to a huge arc above its head, the sudden whiff of its approach, and a distinct feline odor. Before I could collect my senses it turned and dashed across a narrow grassy patch to the edge of a cliff, looked around for a second, and disappeared. We rushed down but all we saw was a blank cliff. The "gray ghost" had vanished.

On reconstructing our encounter, we realized that the leopard had been resting under the overhang where Chhimed stood; when it was disturbed there, it crept down the crest, only to bump into me. Chhimed and I were thrilled beyond words. What a day it was! In celebration, we opened our flask of hot tea and had delicious *pak* (*tsampa*, kneaded with *chhang* and sugar). That evening I acknowledged a newfound adoration for the snow leopard.

I have sighted snow leopards many times since, including one sighting that lasted over nine hours, but this one on Concave Rock stands apart as the most memorable snow leopard sighting, nay, the most memorable wildlife sighting in two decades of work in the Himalaya. Life has moved on since then. I'm fortunate now to work full-time on snow leopard conservation, frequently visiting the alluring white ramparts that framed the northern horizon of my days in the *terai*. My journey from rice fields to snowfields has blessed me with rich experience and passionate, fulfilling work. There are certainly challenges ahead for the snow leopard and the mountains it inhabits, but I'm comforted by the many scientists, managers, and students who have heeded the call to contribute, just as I did twenty years ago. These great mountains seem relatively safe, but continued vigilance and dedicated people are what will keep them from becoming stones of silence.

MITCHELL KELLY

DEATH OF A BHARAL

INDIA—In Ladakh's high mountains, nature's drama of life and death is described in full detail as seen through the lens of a determined filmmaker.

Fly north from Delhi and within an hour you'll be above the peaks of the Indian Himalaya. You'll look down in dread and wonder how an animal can stand upright, let alone survive, and you'll convince yourself that where you're headed couldn't possibly be this rugged. Beneath you the mountains go on and on, and something seems not quite right—you're flying over these peaks, thousands of feet over them, and yet you feel them towering above you. It's your first sense of the power of the Himalaya. The mountains become less white and more brown, and with just the slightest descent you fly between two hills and land at the town of Leh. You'd like a better word than "moonscape" but that's the only one you manage, and at this altitude you care less for description than you do for respiration.

A jeep takes you across the Indus River and up into the mountains until the track runs out, where Namgyal the horseman is waiting for you. Beyond are only foot trails. You'll walk through a cultivated valley and back and forth across the frozen river and, mesmerized by the sound of horse bells, you'll somewhere enter Hemis National Park. The hillsides will steepen to slopes of loose scree and then to cliff, and you'll scan the skyline for animals you can't yet see. Walk like this for half a day and you'll reach a spot where you can no longer call it a valley but rather a canyon: sheer vertical cliff on both sides, a hundred feet apart. Just before you enter the canyon, high up where the scree gives way to cliff, is a spring, flowing warm from the rock for a foot or two before it freezes into a solid ice waterfall. It's one of the few midwinter sources of drinkable water for miles around, the kind of place where you'd expect things to happen. If you're here for months or a year, you'll pass this spot many times, and each time you'll feel the landscape crackle with tension. If you are lucky, it's here that you will meet the snow leopard.

I was here at the invitation of the production company Natural History New Zealand to shoot the Himalayan episode of their latest wildlife series. "Wild Asia: At the Edge" was to show a year in the life of the bharal, the legendary "blue sheep" of the high-altitude mountains. The location was Hemis National Park in Ladakh, India, considered prime snow leopard territory. Although there was no provision in the schedule for dedicated filming of the cats, I immediately agreed to shoot the film. With 160 days of field time, spanning from April 1999 to March 2000, I promised myself I would shoot the very best bharal film I could and trust my conviction that if you spend enough time in a landscape—mindful, alert, respectful time—then wonderful things can happen.

For the next ten months the mountains revealed more amazing things than any one person deserves to see: Tibetan wolves tending their pups at the den, the mayhem of the bharal rut, two cliff-nest golden eagle chicks gorging their way from gonzo to majestic. But the air still pulsed with the absence of the one I had really come to meet, the one that had been lounging around in my psyche ever since I first saw it in a childhood picture book. Whenever possible I'd tracked snow leopards, staked out scrapes and rock scents, even had one near-miss sighting opportunity. From time to time I'd shadowed injured or ill bharal. Although I had managed to get the cats to film themselves with a remote self-triggered camera, I still hadn't actually seen a snow leopard. But late that winter, finally, a limping female bharal I'd been tracking was killed in the night by a snow leopard, ambushed on her way to drink at the ice waterfall. The next morning I set a hide about a hundred feet below the kill and settled in to wait.

As expected, the snow leopard was off the kill, nowhere to be seen. Even though the hide was camouflaged and immobile, everything I'd read on snow leopards suggested that if the cat did return to the carcass, it would be so flighty that I would see it for seconds at best. (I would be ecstatic with that, but I had to remember that I was there to film, not just watch.) To maximize that sighting I needed to predict which direction the leopard would come from. The bharal had been killed on the steep open scree — very exposed — with the only cover the scree's transition to cliff about sixty feet to the left. Below, the scree gave way to the frozen river. I was on the far side of the river, the hide tucked in among bare willow saplings. Too far for my liking, but it was the only workable choice: to feel secure, the snow leopard needed to be higher than my position and separated by a tangible barrier like the river. By focusing on the carcass, then reading the focal length off the side of the lens, I calculated it to be just over a hundred feet away. Which created a dilemma: I felt sure the snow leopard would have taken cover in the cliff to the left. But at that distance I couldn't be sure that the leopard wasn't hunkered down in the scree somewhere near the kill or even lying casually on the stones, right in full view. This was the snow leopard, after all, and after ten months of not finding it I was utterly intimidated by its camouflage.

On the long end of the lens, the bharal was just under full frame. She lay on her right side with all her legs pointing downhill about 300 feet from where I had filmed her the previous evening. It was a classic big-cat kill. Her throat and muzzle were matted with dried saliva from the snow leopard's suffocating bite, and her abdominal cavity was open where the leopard had been feeding. Using the camera as a telescope, I scanned all around her for the snow leopard, scrutinizing the scree in ever-increasing circles for what must have been an hour and a half. No cat. Then I scanned the cliff to the left and found nothing. And so on for the next two hours. I feared the snow leopard had abandoned the kill.

Two magpies found the carcass just after noon. I filmed them hopping in and out of the abdominal cavity, flaunting slivers of viscera in their beaks. Both were vigilant, reorienting to face a new direction every few seconds. Clearly, they had no idea where the leopard was either. It was a ray of hope: if the snow leopard was still around, surely it would act? What cat lets a cocky little bird mess with its food? I got ready to film a charge. But nothing.

At two in the afternoon, shade fell on the bharal. Over at the cliff I heard a rock falling and then another at the edge of the scree, then three more, each closer to the carcass than the last. Through the scrim on the hide window I could make out stones skidding down the slope, from a line progressing toward the kill. But I couldn't see a cat. I thought, "You've got to be kidding." I had a clear line of sight to where something large was moving and dislodging rocks and could have pointed exactly to where I thought it was, but there was nothing there—like the B-movie *Invisible Man*, leaving footprints in the dust and knocking over furniture. My awe of the snow leopard doubled. Then I saw a tail, flicked up in a long arc toward the magpies. A very long, furry tail. Next to it I now saw hindquarters, then the belly and back, next forelegs, and finally the head; as though in plain view, the snow leopard had materialized from rear to front. Like some big fluffy optical illusion, the gross movement of the tail had triggered my brain into learning how to separate the cat from the background. And there it was: a snow leopard.

I swung my lens onto the leopard and started rolling just as it reached the kill, and I saw it had the narrow face of a female. She looked more wild and vulnerable and beautiful than I could ever have prepared myself for, and my breath caught in my throat and tears streamed from my eye straight into my viewfinder, hitting the cold glass and instantly freezing it, ruining my view through the camera. I'd shot about five seconds of once-in-a-lifetime footage, melted at the sight of this feline siren, and blown it. At this stage I still believed the leopard would snatch a mouthful of viscera and flee, so I figured there were just seconds left in the encounter. I quickly defrosted the viewfinder and returned my eye to it, expecting to see, at best, the snow leopard's retreat. But she was still there, poised next to the kill.

She was a large female with a very angry face. She had stayed off the kill until it was no longer in the sun. I figured for fear of over-heating (my hide thermometer, admittedly in shade, read minus 4 degrees Fahrenheit), so watching the magpies bounce around on her dinner all that time must have been driving her crazy. Now she was making up for it. She crouched beside the bharal, fixed one of the magpies with a murderous stare, and exploded out after it with a swipe of her massive paw. Then she spun back around and swatted behind, as if expecting the second magpie to be sneaking a quick peck in her milliseconds absence. She did this three more times, frighteningly fast, but the magpies dodged her so effortlessly that I felt indignant on the snow leopard's behalf. I had come from the "majestic sovereign of the mountains" school of snow leopard adoration, and here she was reduced to a vacuum-activity tantrum by two cheeky and unperturbed magpies. With a peeved expres-sion she lay down behind the length of the dead bharal, her tail tip flicking, then rested her chin on the carcass.

I had filmed it all. Anticipating just a few seconds' glimpse, I had been treated instead to a sustained view not only of a wild snow leopard but also of her interactions with another species. It was beyond what I had hoped for. And she was still there. I began to readjust my expectations. The snow leopard hadn't once looked at the hide, so I was confident she didn't know I was there. With the sun now off the kill, it was possible she would stay with it for the rest of the day. So I allowed myself to hope that I might be able to sit and watch this wild snow leopard for another four hours. That's what the snow leopard does to you: you see it, and it makes you want to see it even more. Not driven but lured.

She sat up behind the kill, looking down-valley. Forelegs straight, head high, in profile she looked like a chunkier cheetah. Everything about her was exquisite, once she lost the peeved expression. I'd expected the snow leopard to be winter gray, but there was a gold tinge to her fur. It matched precisely the dried *Ephedra* shrubs dotted on the scree around her. "Ambush Gold" I decided to name the color. She lifted a paw to rake a few times at the bharal's open abdomen, put her head down, and began to feed. Then, as if she'd forgotten about them, the snow leopard snapped back up and snarled at the magpies. They hadn't moved, but she snarled anyway. She pushed her head into the abdominal cavity and ate. It looked dainty, although all I could see was the top of her head bobbing. When she lifted it again to eyeball the magpies, a hand-sized piece of dark red organ hung from her jaws, and her cheeks and the bridge of her nose were painted red with blood. The bharal looked peaceful lying there on its side, asleep almost. I had known her yesterday, alive and coherent. Now she was moving in other directions.

Suddenly, the snow leopard tensed, stopped eating, and flattened onto the rocks. A red fox had appeared and was orbiting the kill. It was young and bushy, bright ginger, utterly lovely. The snow leopard fixed it with a look of terrifying malevolence, a stare you wouldn't want to be at the end of. She was flat, wired, an attack posture with every muscle humming. Unlike her response to the magpies, which had seemed more a venting of frustration at an animal she knew she was unlikely to catch, it seemed that the snow leopard genuinely wanted to murder the fox and genuinely believed she could. Perhaps she'd lost a cub once, killed or scavenged by a fox. Or had too many meals ruined by its attentions: you want to keep your kill for yourself, and if it's a gray animal on gray scree and you are perfectly camouflaged yourself, you don't appreciate a bouncy little ginger fox advertising the spot to nearby wolves, dhole (wild dog), or other snow leopards. Or was it just that the fox was large and slow enough to be in the snow leopard's "things to kill and eat" category? I didn't know. The scenes before me had already moved beyond what I had read about the wild snow leopard. All I could do now was extrapolate from experiences with, and readings about, other cats, other carnivores. I was in the exhilarating position of working it out as I went along.

I thought the snow leopard would charge the fox. She didn't. The fox was too cautious to get within range. It sniffed the air, trotted a few feet, then sniffed again, all the way around the leopard on her kill. Pressed in among the scree stones, the leopard had disappeared but for the smear of red blood on her nose and cheeks. This was the snow leopard as ambush predator: controlled, focused, infinitely patient. The rock that leaps. I was willing that delightful little fox not to get too close when the magpies, oblivious to the drama of it all, decided this was an excellent time to pull the snow leopard's tail.

I had seen them do this before, with the tail of a wolf and the tail feathers of a lammergeyer, and later that day I would see them do it to the fox. The magpie would sneak half forward, half sideways up to the tip of the tail, take a beak-full of fur (or feathers), and tug. The wolf had snapped, the lammergeyer had snapped, and the fox endured four hearty tugs before snapping too. Evidently, this was a tired old game that also included the snow leopard. She spun around swatting at the magpie, which dodged her swipes and casually flew back to chatter with its mate. Hunched and peeved, the snow leopard had blown her ambush posture. The magpies never removed fur or feathers when doing this (unlike during the bharal summer molt when there was no doubt they were collecting nest-lining hair from the bharals' backs). Perhaps the behavior is a prompt: the four animals I'd seen them tail-pull were all capable of opening carcasses, so could it be that the magpies pulled tails whenever they grew impatient with that animal's inactivity? Once the animal eats, the magpies get scraps. Had the magpies used a quick tail-tug to change snow leopard the mighty ambush predator into snow leopard the utilitarian can opener?

The snow leopard was peeved again but dozy, too, from feeding. She stretched out lengthwise behind the bharal, almost spooning the carcass. She rested her head on the nape of the bharal's neck, and her eyelids were heavy. I'd seen this with other big cats, what seemed a sensual connection to the dead prey, beyond the eating. For the first time she looked satisfied.

I'd kept the lens on the snow leopard since she first appeared, as I still wasn't sure I could find her again if she were to relocate slightly and blend back into the rocks when I wasn't looking. I film with my right eye on the viewfinder, looking through the camera, and my left eye open to monitor the surrounding activity, which means each eye is on a different focal length. You can get a blinding headache fast this way, so you need to give your camera eye a rest from time to time if you want to last the day.

I felt comfortable spotting the snow leopard when she was moving, but I urgently needed to build confidence in finding her when she was still. While she dozed I finally had time to study her camouflage. Her basic coat color ranged from off-white on her underside up to the gentle gold on her shoulders, back, and haunches. Her rosettes and facial markings were black. There was actually very little gray anywhere on her coat, but the superimposition of black spots over pale undercoat created an impression of mid-tone that matched precisely the pervasive gray of the landscape (remembering that all of her mammalian prey saw only in black and white). The bharal, who actually are the same allover mid-gray as the rocks, are hard enough to spot, but the snow leopard refined it further: her black rosettes mimicked the dark shadows under every rock and stone, totally breaking up her outline. That was how she "disappeared" when still, but it was also something I could work with: her rosettes were ever so slightly smaller and closer together than the scree shadows. By not looking for the shape the brain registered as "leopard" but instead for an irregular clumping of slightly smaller black "shadows," I could find her again relatively easily. It helped to squint (this crushes the colors and enhances the contrast), and I wondered if this was why most snow leopard sightings happen in the half-light of dawn and dusk rather than being purely an indication of activity patterns, as previously believed. (Over the next few years my faith in this theory grew as I watched snow leopards moving at all times of day, in winter at least). Most camouflage is a compromise — very few animals live in a landscape uniform across all terrains and all seasons — so I was about to dismiss her off-white base color as a concession to the snows of winter when I realized that, by being so pale, her base coat was actually picking up a lot of reflected light.

Put a sheet of white paper next to a red chair, and you'll notice that the paper now looks slightly red, as it reflects back the color of the chair. It's just physics; the paper hasn't changed at all. Try it now with black paper: still a hint of red, but barely. So the snow leopard's pale undercoat allows her to take on something of the tone and color of whatever surface she is on. It's a very subtle effect, but when combined with the outline disruption of the black rosettes, it gives her camouflage a greater potency and versatility than the bharals' rock-matching solid gray, which works only well for them when they are actually on those rocks. (Or hillsides— the bharals' hair color drifts with the landscape to brownish by midsummer, then back to slate gray by winter.) Realizing this effect of reflected light, I now understood why I had trouble pinning down the snow leopard's exact color in the first hours after she appeared. Near the dried *Ephedra* bushes she had seemed golden, but over the scree she appeared gray. Ironically, the snow leopard's camouflage is least effective in snow. As I learned over the next few years, a sighting of this spotted cat on a landscape of white is the easiest you'll get. Although studying her while she dozed meant my camera eye didn't get a rest, this impromptu course in snow leopard camouflage was time well spent. It enabled me to relax slightly, to wallow in the wildness of it all without the relentless anxiety of having the snow leopard suddenly vanish.

When the snow leopard finished dozing, the magpies were still watching her and the fox was still orbiting and something far up-valley had caught her attention, something she wasn't happy about. She had made the kill in a very exposed place, and now she wanted the carcass off the scree and into the cover of the cliff. Standing upslope, she took the bharal by the throat and tugged backward. Nothing. She dug her hind paws in among the scree and tugged again. On the third tug the carcass moved a few inches, then jammed on the stones. The snow leopard really dug in now, her hindquarters scrambling sideways trying to find purchase on the loose scree, in an arc to the left then an arc to the right, her jaws on the throat as the pivot, her ears pinned back, and her long tail stiff and pumping like a lever. This moved the bharal a few more inches, but she was dislodging too many stones down the slope, creating too much commotion. She gave up. The bharal was too heavy for her to drag. She would need to eat a lot more of it before trying again. She lay back down, resigned to the magpies and the fox, and whatever had bothered her up-valley eventually moved on.

So it went until dusk. The snow leopard fed, rested, tried to murder the magpies. She sat and cleaned the blood from her face with a paw. She looked menacing. She looked huggable. She had surprised me all day. Within minutes of meeting her, the mystical, mysterious, ghostlike snow leopard had begun to transform into a very real, very peeved big cat just trying to protect her dinner.

In the last light she left the kill and sauntered off up the cliff toward the spring to drink. I had watched her all day, and back at camp in my sleeping bag a few hours later, I shut my eyes and watched her all night too, not sleeping a wink. I'd been gifted with an opportunity to meet the snow leopard on her own terms, to let the cat emerge from the metaphor and legend and just be the animal she is. In front of me on that mountainside, unshackled from all I'd read and watched and heard, the snow leopard had snapped into clear focus. I now knew she was real and that the mountains were healthy.

When I returned the next morning she was still there, and again the day after that. For those three days I tried to film everything the snow leopard did, to let her tell her own story through her actions and inactions. After two days of feeding, she lost the kill overnight to a large male snow leopard, and midway through that third day he dragged the carcass high up the mountainside to a rocky crag, where he and the magpies fed under a light snowfall. I sat in the hide with the male snow leopard to my left, the female to my right, feeling lucky, greedy, euphoric. On the fourth day both snow leopards had moved on, and it was unbearably lonely. What remained of the carcass was pecked at by a flock of thirty yellow-billed choughs. Only on the fifth day did vultures dare land to feed on the remains, convinced at last that the leopards were gone. The last footage I took of the bharal, which I had first filmed six days earlier limping across the scree, was of her foreleg being swallowed whole by a lammergeyer—skin, hair, bones, and all. And then the mountainside was still. The bharal had become snow leopard, fox, magpie, vulture.

Within a year I was back to shoot a second film on the snow leopards. Of all the creatures in the world, I chose to see them again. Who can say why some animals exhilarate us more than others? Once you meet them in the mountains, you are beguiled forever. They are wild, beautiful, imperfect, and real. They are the best of this earth. They are the snow leopards.

AVAANTSEREN BAYARJARGAL

AN ACCORD OF HOPE

MONGOLIA—*This teacher-cum–snow leopard conservationist shares her experiences in changing the attitudes of local people who share the world of the snow leopard.*

I began my career as a language teacher in the northern province of Mongolia called Khuvsgul, never imagining that someday I would become deeply connected to the snow leopard. My lucky break came out of the blue when I was asked to translate for a research team from the United States that was just beginning a study of snow leopards in the Gobi Altai, Mongolia. This chance opportunity opened a new career that allowed me to involve local people in an innovative conservation scheme to protect the snow leopards of my country. In ten years of active conservation work, I've never seen a snow leopard in the wild, yet my heart beats a closeness with this rare cat.

Part of my new job was to translate the responses of local herders interviewed by the snow leopard research team. The attitudes of local people toward this natural predator dominated the interviews. There were no snow leopards where I grew up in northern Mongolia, so the responses both educated and touched me. After hundreds of interviews, some common themes surfaced: most herding families subsisted on less than one dollar per day and the snow leopards menaced their lives, killing precious livestock. Local people often trapped and killed them as a consequence.

My firsthand immersion into local people's difficult lives and my growing empathy for the snow leopard caused me to think deeply about the future of both. Fortunately, other good minds were focused on the same dilemma. Together, we framed an incentive-based conservation scheme that tied snow leopard survival to raising the standard of living of local herders. The idea centered on encouraging local women to spin yarn and teaching them to make handicrafts that would be sold internationally by the Snow Leopard Trust, a US-based nongovernmental organization. Under the scheme, all proceeds from the sales would return to the participating families, including a twenty-percent bonus for protecting the snow leopard. A single violation by anyone in the community would cause the bonus to be forfeited. I am privileged to share some personal accounts of how this program played out in real life.

Tulgazana Darikhuu lives in the southern Gobi region of Mongolia; like others in the area, the family's livelihood depends entirely on raising livestock. Of middle age with five children, Tulgazana lives a nomadic existence, seasonally changing locations for better grazing. This means he must move his home, the highly versatile and mobile ger (Mongolian traditional felt tent), several times a year, just as generations before him have done. In the area where Tulgazana lives, most herders have goats, sheep, and a few domestic Bactrian camels. Fiercely independent, Mongolian nomads are drawn to a remote, difficult lifestyle that makes it hard to access social services and fair markets for livestock products such as raw wool. Too often, they must rely on middlemen who circuit nomadic communities, paying less than fair value for goods.

Tulgazana grazes his stock on mountainsides and valleys shared by local wildlife, such as marmots and wild sheep and goats—the snow leopard's natural prey. Either because of hunger or opportunity, snow leopards occasionally take livestock, the lifeblood of local people already on the margins of survival. In this world of no crops and little, if any, outside income, it is impossible to overstate the value of family livestock in sustaining life on the Mongolian steppe. When we first interviewed Tulgazana, he had just lost several sheep to snow leopards. Not surprisingly, he and his wife viewed the snow leopard as an enemy. From footprints on fresh snow beside the carcasses, he figured there were three cats: one adult and two cubs. They had killed but not eaten the dead sheep, enraging Tulgazana and causing him to want to seek revenge on these killers. He set traps, but after days and days of tending them, he gave up. His failure brought embarrassment, as the other herders in his community watched and hoped for his success in ridding them of the killer beasts.

In March the following year (2000) I got to know Tulgazana better when he and his wife, Sarantsetseg, and their neighbors were invited to a community to learn about a training program. Such events rarely happen in remote areas, so they were keen to learn what this training was about. They set out to the meeting astride their small two-cylinder motorcycle. The meeting focused on how to involve local people in snow leopard conservation—an unimaginable concept to Tulgazana and the others at the meeting. He thought to himself, "Don't these people know we hate the snow leopard, that it kills our stock and steals from our meager existence?" Nonetheless, those conducting the training taught the women to make felt toys and instructed them about delivery in spring of the following year. The meeting launched the beginning of our program, a bold experiment to find accord between humans and leopards.

The cycle continued, modestly at first but growing each year. Each spring the homemade goods were collected and the funds dispersed to each household. Sarantsetseg learned how to spin camel yarn and bought a spinning wheel with a micro-credit loan through the program. She learned to knit camel wool mittens and spin yarn into skeins, which bring a much better price than raw wool. From only a few extra dollars the first year, her production and income increased as her skills improved, adding precious extra cash for family needs. Slowly, the couple began to think differently about the snow leopard, since its conservation was the central reason for their good fortune. Over time, Tulgazana and Sarantsetseg grew to enjoy and appreciate the program, wanting it to continue indefinitely.

Tulgazana writes as a hobby. To his great joy and amazement, the snow leopard opened doors for his writing and challenged his commitment to its conservation. He started by writing for our newsletter. Small stories at first, but, like Sarantsetseg, he honed his skills and became interested in learning more about the snow leopard. He studied all aspects of snow leopards, learning about their movement, their prey, how they hunt, and so forth, until he could write with authority about this rare cat. Tulgazana's excitement about snow leopards showed in his writing, which conveyed wonderful messages to the community. From a newsletter to the provincial daily paper to a published compilation of stories, *Snow Leopards in Noyon*, Tulgazana's stories evoked empathy for a cat once loathed by him and many others.

In addition to his writing, Tulgazana became a volunteer ranger and a local educator on wildlife conservation. His interaction with neighbors and other herders helped him see the importance of conservation education. He took his conservation message to local schools, setting up children's clubs to work on nature education.

In the winter, Tulgazana lost about 75 of his 250 stock to predators, including snow leopards. In the face of this horrific loss, he held no animosity for the cat; rather, he expressed interest in getting a remote camera so he could report more accurately about stock raiding in the newspaper. He worried about the reaction of other herders who lost livestock that winter. Not wanting the revenge mentality to return, as he had only a few years earlier, he talked one-on-one with his neighbors, encouraging tolerance and urging them to support a new stock insurance program that would compensate losses from predators. What an incredible journey for Tulgazana and Sarantsetseg. Their story shows how a small incentive and education lead to changed attitudes that improve the odds for snow leopard survival.

My second story begins with the death of Longtail, a radio-collared snow leopard that lived in the Tost Mountain range of Gurvantes County, South Gobi—about 60 miles from where Tulgazana lives. This long-term study received the blessing of locals, largely because of the success of our incentive program. A local herder shot Longtail, claiming to have lost twenty-six goats to predators in previous weeks. Around 1:00 one morning he heard an animal trying to enter his corral. Attempting to scare it away, he shot blindly several times in the direction of the noise. A couple of days later he found Longtail dead, about one mile from his ger. Realizing the deadly consequences of his actions, he was faced with having to inform the researchers and his community.

His careless shooting cost the community its 20 percent conservation bonus. The local women, obviously unhappy about the incident, took their discontent directly to the herder, demanding that he pay the bonus. The poor herder did not have the money, but he promised never to harm a snow leopard again, acknowledging the loss he had caused to so many families. Longtail's death marked the first and only forfeit of the conservation bonus caused by an incident involving the snow leopard. (In western Mongolia a poached red deer triggered the loss of the bonus. Here again, upset women in the program sought reimbursement directly from the poacher.) Longtail's death brought much sadness but rallied critical thinking about how to coexist with snow leopards, prompting a series of workshops for herders to convey their thoughts on ways to prevent further losses. Foremost, they felt that compensation for loss of livestock would help. They eventually adopted a community-based insurance scheme similar to successful programs in India.

My final story is about Sainbileg Yungee, one of many rural women who found empowerment by participating in conservation activities and helping others understand the importance of conservation. The appointment of local coordinators selected by the community grew out of our program. These women receive a small stipend for their role as advisers, trainers, and coordinators. Sainbileg is coordinator for Yamaat Valley in Uvs, western Mongolia. Yamaat Valley provides habitat for a wide rage of wildlife, including the snow leopard. Sainbileg has four children between the ages of five and eighteen. Her husband, Erdenebaatar, works as a ranger for the Turgen Mountain Protected Area. Her youngest child lives at home; the three older children go to provincial school eighty miles away. Erdenebaatar's salary is insufficient to support the family, so their primary income comes from their herds of sheep and yak. With Erdenebaatar busy patrolling the park, most of the herding responsibility falls on Sainbileg. She was selected as the county coordinator because most of the other local women felt her husband's job made her better qualified and more knowledgeable about conservation. Turns out, they were right.

Like her neighbors, she knew nothing about modern methods for processing wool. With training, she learned quickly and soon became a teacher in her community and used her skills to find ways to improve the quality of products for her area. Erdenebaatar became a community voice for conservation at the same time. Admittedly, early on the new revenue stream from handicrafts sold under the program kept them interested. Over time, however, as Sainbileg realized that the program was for the long term, her attitude shifted from just making extra money to understanding the larger picture of snow leopard and human interaction. Modest added revenue granted an atmosphere of tolerance and understanding and fostered a true sense of empowerment. Self-confidence and expanded knowledge about conservation led her to organize a local cooperative of thirteen households focused on improving land-use practices. With Erdenebaatar and Sainbileg's leadership, the community realized a newfound strength through working together. Like it did for Tulgazana and Sarantsetseg, the snow leopard led them to a new place in their lives. It is a life they now share willingly with the snow leopard, a rare cat that in many ways symbolizes their own existence.

I hope my stories touched your heart, just as meeting these wonderful people touched my heart. In their lives, their empathy, and their caring actions, I find hope in the possibility of a lasting accord between humans and leopards.

A S H I Q   A H M A D   K H A N

TEARS OF THE KARAKORUM

PAKISTAN—*A young girl's grief becomes the guiding light for a wildlife manger driven to find a way for humans and snow leopards to coexist.*

August 1982. I left camp at dawn, awed by the morning sun reflecting off the snowy white peaks of the Karakorum range that engulfed me. Cool, crisp mountain air held spirits high as young legs eagerly took to the trail in search of the rare Marco Polo sheep. I had been in these mountains before, but on the trail out of camp I realized that I knew little of this iconic bighorn sheep named after the famous Venetian explorer who opened Europe's eyes to the wonder and grandeur of central Asia. In Pakistan they live on the high shoulders of the Karakorum Mountains, a range that boasts sixty peaks above 23,000 feet—including K2, the second-highest mountain in the world. It had been a wish, a dream, to see these magnificent animals someday. A smile framed my face this glorious morning, as I realized it was now my job as wildlife specialist for the Pakistan Forest Institute to study these remarkable animals. With each step up the rugged trails toward the high grazing slopes, my excitement welled up just imagining a glimpse of this rare animal. My accompanying wildlife watcher had warned earlier that it was rare to actually see one in this location, but my strong desire could not be quelled.

After an hour or so we caught a distant view of several herders' huts, with smoke coming from one of them. I thought to myself, "If people are about, how could the illusive Marco Polo be nearby?" My hopes began to fade, knowing that if there were sheep about, they would be at least an hour or more away. With this in mind, we moved toward the huts to seek the herders' opinion about where the sheep might be.

As we approached the huts, an unexpected scene unfolded. A small family of meager means was mourning the loss of dead and injured sheep in the corral. An elderly man, perhaps the owner or tender, though visibly upset himself, comforted a little girl barely five years old who was openly sobbing. Tears streamed down her reddened cheeks. One of the dead lambs had been her pet. As is the case with most children in herding families, the daily interaction with livestock from birth creates close bonds, filling lonely days with fun and companionship. Others in the family roamed the corral aimlessly, their sad and empty faces overwhelmed by the loss.

Confused, I couldn't image what animal could have done such a thing — wolves, leopards, or some new predator unfamiliar to me. The herder family, however, knew with absolute certainty what had perpetrated this horrible carnage — it was a snow leopard. I knew nothing about snow leopards, having only seen one in the zoo. The death and emotional distress before my astonished eyes caused me to immediately frame an opinion of this night stalker: a cruel animal of no use, a killer of the domestic livestock of poor people, rendering them even poorer. Bleeding animals and a little girl's tears moved me to join hands with the family in a wish to eliminate such animals altogether. Thoughts of Marco Polo sheep evaporated among these good people's anguish.

My life and career would forever circle back to this unfortunate incident in the high Karakorum. I learned that, over the years, local people had cleverly devised a number of techniques to kill snow leopards. Villages also accepted the "help" of outsiders who would kill snow leopards, taking the luxuriant pelt in exchange. The herders had no idea what eventually happened to the pelts but focused only on the relief of another stock killer gone. Thus, I became convinced that locals were in some ways better equipped than I, a neophyte biologist, for dealing with snow leopards. They were more familiar with their habits; they knew how to use poisons and traps; and, if they had guns, they knew how to shoot them. It seemed there was no place for snow leopards in their world. I lacked the skills to reconcile the situation. I felt helpless.

The more I learned about the herders' conflict with snow leopards, the more convinced I became that a solution must be found. Simultaneously, I needed to learn more about snow leopards so I could devise plausible management approaches to teach to my forestry students. Rather than enlightened, however, I became more confused as I studied snow leopard distribution, life history, prey regulation, and legal status. My confusion led to serious thought about what might work. I thought of a scheme for compensating herders for lost livestock, but I had no idea how to make such a program actually work.

I also thought about trophy hunting but needed to reconcile in my own heart this rather conflicting approach to conservation. The more I saw hunters killing native animals and birds, the more I disliked hunting altogether. The vainglorious stories of hunter "successes" left me cold. My internal debate was agonizing, but I finally reconciled my feelings, knowing that hunting goes on and profits go to a privileged few. It was a difficult decision to promote something I disliked, but I became consumed with finding a way to shift the focus to conservation and to direct the profits—at least a portion of them—to the impoverished local people.

The opportunity to test trophy hunting came in 1989 when I found myself back in the Karakorum, this time to motivate local villagers to protect Himalayan ibex. Ibex were abundant in the rich pastures of the mountain slopes, but a few local hunters—perhaps only eleven or so—kept the population from flourishing. Few animals survived for ten years. Further, it wasn't meat for the pot; these hunters used the meat for gifting. After months of tedious negotiations, I convinced the entire community of villagers to abide by one simple rule: protect the ibex until there are enough in number and size to sustain a trophy-hunting program for foreign hunters. The government would run the program and return 75 percent of the income generated back to the community. This was the beginning of a journey that would prove to be long and tiring, but one that held great promise for the future of wildlife in northern Pakistan. Though not entirely new, trophy hunting combined with community participation had gained sporadic acceptance in some commercial cases and national parks. For me, it began in Bar Valley in the Nagar Sub Division of the newly created province of Gilgit-Baltistan.

My standing agreement, negotiated personally with the village elders of Bar Valley, did not directly address the snow leopard; however, the residents did practice a degree of snow leopard conservation. Initially, noncompliance with the rule was kept at a low profile, meaning I overlooked some violations to give the process a chance. But as the social improvements built into our agreement materialized, the community self-enforced more stringent adherence to the rule. By the mid-1990s the incentive-based approach to wildlife conservation, including trophy hunting, had become increasingly popular, leading to more sophisticated and transparent agreements that also included provisions for protecting all wildlife—including snow leopards.

A second opportunity to use a community participation model came when I was asked to write a management plan for the newly created Khunjerab National Park (KNP), located on Pakistan's northern border with China. KNP is richly blessed with diverse wildlife, including Marco Polo sheep, ibex, and snow leopard. Grazing disputes, however, prevented KNP from realizing its full potential as a haven for wildlife. My job was to write a management plan that would resolve the grazing conflict, recognizing that local people held centuries-old grazing rights. It took three long years to reach a consensual agreement. But with community support, the plan began showing results from the start. Sheep and ibex numbers grew rapidly and these animals were often visible from the road.

Ibex flourished, not just in the park but in adjacent areas as well, where trophy hunting continues to this day. Further, the prevailing attitude toward conservation included snow leopards in spite of continued livestock raiding. I learned of several incidents where snow leopards were released from corrals with injured sheep still bleeding. In addition to the conservation conditions included in the management plan, snow leopards benefited indirectly from trophy hunting, which funded village-wide benefits—such as improved bridges, irrigation canals, and schools. Thus village-wide sentiment to protect snow leopards trumped the anger of a single villager's loss. In spite of improved conditions for the snow leopard, my personal interactions with livestock owners convinced me that village pressure could only go so far in preventing retaliatory killings.

The question of what to do continued to bother me until I came across a case history of Ayubia National Park. Communities living in the park's buffer zone accepted the loss of livestock taking by common leopards in exchange for compensation from a livestock insurance scheme run by the community but initially facilitated by an impartial outside agency. Each livestock owner paid annual fees on a per-head basis into the insurance fund. With good management the fund grew, making it possible to compensate actual losses to leopards. The program later spread to three sites that have the snow leopard, one in the Hindu Kush and two in the Karakorum. Over the past five years, there have been no reports of snow leopard deaths as a result of retaliation killing or reports of poaching for the felt and bone trade. Trophy hunting, combined with an insurance scheme, seems to hold great promise for long-term protection of the snow leopard. Time will tell.

Today, I'm not fully satisfied that there aren't other, less invasive approaches to help snow leopards and local people coexist. I continue to explore new models in which the revenue from trophy hunting is replaced by eco-tourism, medicinal plant collection, or honey and fruit production. I look forward to the day when I can replace the slogan "money for conservation" with "money without killing." My passion and persistence for conservation rest on a foundation of association with good organizations and friends with big hearts and beautiful minds. I prize my closeness to dozens of herder communities, and I'm proud to have so many loving friends of different races and religions who share the vision of a promising future. Good people become assets and helping hands in the conservation journey—a journey with no obvious end. For me, one thing is certain: my journey will always honor the tears of a little girl in the high Karakorum.

S H A F Q A T   H U S S A I N

THE PELT SMUGGLER

PAKISTAN—*In trying to do the right thing, two colleagues must embark on a journey filled with danger and intrigue until the final moment.*

It was the winter of 1999. My assistant, Ghulam Mohammad (GM), and I had just completed our first in a series of surveys in northern Pakistan's Baltistan region. Earlier in the year I had received a small grant from a London-based conservation organization to look into the possibility of starting an insurance scheme for domestic livestock against snow leopard predation. The idea was to protect the snow leopard against the retaliatory actions of angry villagers who had lost livestock to them. In gathering ethnographic and biological data, we conducted surveys in four valleys across Baltistan. GM and I were the core survey team, together with a number of porters to carry our supplies.

December 22—the day after we returned to Skardu (the principal town in Baltistan) from our first survey—was cold, dark, and still. I stayed in a guest house run by an enterprising local elite who, more than monetary gain, sought to provide more cosmopolitan accommodations than were otherwise available in this small town nestled high in the Karakorum Mountains.

At about 4:00 p.m. GM appeared with one of the porters who had accompanied us on the survey. I was surprised to see the porter, as I thought he had returned to his village after the survey ended. I welcomed them inside for a cup of tea. GM is at once a serious and innocent-looking fellow, eager but also proud and always seeking opportunities to do the right thing. The porter was a young Shina who spoke Balti. I had forgotten his name, so, mimicking foreign trekkers who call all Balti men Ali, I asked, "So, Ali, how are you doing?" He remained quiet and tried to smile, but then his expression became regretful, even painful. I asked if he was tired from the trip and if he would like to accompany us on the next survey. He remained quiet. I turned to GM who was shifting uncomfortably in his chair, looking as if he was preparing to say something. He said quietly and rather disdainfully that "Ali" did not understand Urdu, shaking his head as if to say that it was not just Urdu that the porter did not understand. I was confused by his slightly hostile tone and sensed that this was more than just a polite visit, that something more than coincidence had brought them to my lodging.

I asked GM to tell me what was going on. He reached into his rucksack and, with a struggle, pulled out a tightly wrapped package stuffed inside the plastic sacking of a fertilizer commonly used in the region. To my great surprise, he unfolded the wrapping to reveal a snow leopard pelt folded into a tight ball. He looked at me and then at Ali. "Where did it come from?" I asked. "From Hushey," GM replied, "the village through which we passed on our way to and from the survey we just completed." "But how?" I asked, still confused as to what exactly was going on. "He says he bought it for us," said GM. "What?" I asked, in both shock and anger. "Yeeaas," said GM, slightly elongating the "yes" to express his anger.

GM explained that Ali had been under the impression that I was a snow leopard smuggler from the Punjab and that I was visiting the area to collect pelts from the region. He knew we had presented ourselves as conservationists but had taken this to be a cover for our real intentions. Thinking he could profit from the situation, Ali had secretly bought a pelt from a local farmer for 8,000 rupees as we passed through Hushey on our way back from the survey and was now trying to sell it to us for 16,000 rupees. For a moment I thought I was a victim of a Balti version of Candid Camera. But there was no other hidden plot to be exposed; what had already been exposed was explosive enough. I was not sure whether to be angry with Ali for his stupidity or to pity him. I was totally confused as to how he could have concluded that we were looking for snow leopard pelts. His facial expression indicated not simply that he regretted having come to the wrong conclusion about our intentions but also that he was wondering why we would want to protect such a useless animal, particularly when a tidy profit could be made from its pelt.

I began to realize that Ali still wasn't fully convinced that he had misunderstood anything. Our logic and worldviews were incommensurable, it seemed. Looking back on the situation later, I began to wonder, was Ali's behavior really that unreasonable? Was it so surprising that he had concluded that I was seeking to buy pelts? In retrospect, I think that as far as misunderstandings go, this one was the most likely to happen. It is a well-known fact that outside traders often secretly buy snow leopard pelts from local farmers. Even national and international trekkers and tourists sometimes ask about pelts. The supply of pelts and wildlife products has a unique history in the region. During the height of the Victorian era in the late nineteenth century, Baltistan was very popular among sportsmen. Often, if their hunting had been unsuccessful, they would buy trophies from local hunters and pass them off as their own. So Ali was not that much off the mark when he mistook us for modern-day trophy hunters.

At the time, however, I was still in shock and not sure how to handle the situation. I began to yell at Ali, telling him he had committed a very serious crime and could end up in jail, though I did this mainly to scare him; I had no intention of putting the poor fellow behind bars. At the same time, I wondered if I should report the matter to the Office of the Divisional Forester, thinking that otherwise the misunderstanding could gain more traction and

I might end up in jail myself. I asked GM what to do. We could not let Ali take the pelt because he would sell it to someone else, or even worse, he might be discovered and his act attached to our project and our names. But keeping the pelt meant we would be stuck with it, and we might be discovered and be accused of trading in pelts. If we turned the pelt over to the authorities in Skardu, poor Ali would be in terrible trouble. Both the reputation of our budding project and Ali's backside were on the line. GM and I thought hard; Ali sat there half sulking, half bored. Finally, we decided to "confiscate" the pelt. We told Ali that we would keep the pelt but that we intended to destroy it and we would not report him to the police. He began to protest, saying we needed to pay him, that he had spent a great deal of money buying the pelt. We reminded him that if we told the authorities, he would find himself in a great deal of trouble, and he left, grumbling. (We did later arrange for him to be partially compensated for his loss.)

GM and I began to discuss our options for disposing of the pelt. We spread it out on the floor and examined it. It was a fully preserved pelt of a seven- or eight-year-old female. It had been trapped using a leg snare, clear from the very distinct circular mark of the metal trap on the front left leg. The skinning had been done with care and precision. This showed, rather alarmingly, that whoever had prepared it was an expert. One of the front canine teeth was broken, and all the paws were missing; I suspected that they had been sent to China, where they likely fetched a good price for use in Chinese medicine.

That evening GM's older brother Mehdi joined us. Mehdi is a jack-of-all-trades kind of guy. He runs a successful catering business in Skardu, rubbing shoulders with high dignitaries, and his unabashed confidence reflected that experience. Mehdi had been made aware of the issue and had come to learn the final verdict. He was relieved to find out that we had decided not to report the matter but was bemused by the fact that we were stuck with the pelt. The irony of the situation was not lost on any of us: snow leopard conservationists were in possession of an illegal snow leopard pelt.

Mehdi suggested that we take the pelt to a lake outside the town and burn it, but GM and I were averse to the idea. The specimen we had was in very good condition, and we had begun to wonder if we might be able to create something positive out of the situation by doing something worthwhile with the pelt. It was getting too late to think clearly. The fire in the stove was dwindling, and the temperature was falling sharply. Mehdi went out into the cold and came back with his arms full of wood. He filled the stove as I wrapped myself in three layers of blankets, took a last peek at the pelt, and closed my eyes.

The next day I visited an old forester friend, Jawad Ali, who worked for a rural development organization. I found him smoking a cigarette and drinking a cup of tea. Another man was sitting at his desk, also drinking tea. I recognized him from steering committee meetings. He was Nawab Zaheer, a Pashtun tribal leader and a passionate conservationist. He is respected among government and nongovernment organization staff alike for his inspirational work and his open and frank criticism. I explained my predicament and asked for their advice. Jawad looked puzzled, but Nawab seemed unimpressed by the gravity of the situation. He told me calmly that he had recently visited the Pakistan Natural History Museum in Islamabad and noticed that it was missing specimens of many species from the country's northern areas. He offered to talk to the director of the museum and ask if they would accept a snow leopard pelt from me. I was more than relieved to hear Nawab's suggestion and at once accepted his offer. He called Islamabad, explained the situation to the director, and asked if he could use the pelt for the museum. Nawab thanked the director and put down the phone. "Good news," he said. "The director will take the pelt without asking any questions. He is a very practical man." I thanked Nawab profusely and asked when I could bring him the pelt to take to Islamabad. He looked irritated. "I've shown you the way," he said. "Now it's up to you to tread the path."

Two days had passed since the pelt had come into our possession. Taking it to Islamabad, more than 600 miles away, seemed like an impossible task. I could certainly not take the pelt on a plane, as it would likely be detected in the pre-flight security search and would probably lead to my arrest. Taking it by road on the Karakoram Highway (KKH) was the only realistic option. This, too, was risky, however, since the KKH between Skardu and Islamabad has about two dozen police, customs, and forest check posts. Taking the pelt on the road would amount to running the literal and metaphorical gauntlet. GM and Mehdi suggested that it would be less risky to travel with the pelt in a private vehicle than using public transport, as the latter is subject to frequent checks and inspections. Jawad suggested that we hire a private jeep and pretend to be tourists from Punjab.

Early Christmas morning, GM, Mehdi, and I set out for Islamabad in a rented vehicle. The pelt was tightly packed inside my small rucksack, which was packed in a larger rucksack and placed at the bottom of the luggage. Mehdi had sprinkled the rucksack with dry flour as a ceremonial gesture of protection against potential harm, bad omens, and danger. I had been rehearsing in my mind various scenarios and possible explanations in case we were caught by authorities. I had taken down the telephone number of the director of the museum in case I had to call him to verify my story that the pelt was not intended for personal collection but was heading to the museum.

The sixteen-hour journey began well. The first army check post right outside Skardu was unmanned, and we cruised through the following three check posts without being searched. At noon we reached Gilgit, where we had lunch. The road between Gilgit and Islamabad goes through some of the wildest country in the Himalayas. Highway robberies and sectarian killings had rendered the road dangerous, hence the presence of patrol vehicles and check posts. We left after lunch, thinking about the next potentially threatening check post at Chilas, the next district south of Gilgit. As we crossed the district boundary we approached a long, stationary queue of vehicles, with passengers sitting about and strolling along the road. At the front of the queue was a contingent of policemen doing a random security check of vehicles. Cold sweat ran down my forehead on that cool December afternoon. GM announced that this was it, our fate had been sealed, and soon we would be behind bars. Mehdi scolded his younger brother for being so ready to give in. He took a bundle of rupee notes out of his wallet and put them in his shirt pocket. I searched for anything that might prove that I was a snow leopard conservationist rather than a pelt smuggler. About fifteen minutes later two policemen dawdled past our vehicle. We gave them a nervous smile. They smiled back and greeted us politely. They asked where I was from and requested to see my national identification card. They then asked the same from GM and Mehdi. While we were proving our identities, one of the policemen circled back to the trunk of the jeep and looked at our luggage. He asked if we had been camping. I told him I was a snow leopard conservationist and had been doing surveys. He seemed satisfied. Our interrogation was over. We crossed the check post and for the next three hours, until the next check post in Kohistan, pondered the many scenarios that might have unfolded if the pelt had been found.

I was not too worried about the material consequences of being caught smuggling the pelt, as I would likely have been able to pull strings to get out of any legal trouble, but the symbolic damage to my work and reputation weighed heavily on my mind. Moreover, being caught in a remote town by a smalltime policeman, who was not sure of his powers or those of his subject, would not have been a pleasant experience. I have been stopped at check posts many times and seen how police and authorities can become predatory.

We crossed two more check posts, where we were minimally questioned and our luggage ceremonially searched. As we crossed each check post our confidence grew and the search process became less stressful. The final search was conducted when we were entering Islamabad at the stroke of midnight. We pulled into a local hotel and checked into our rooms. Tired and hungry, we asked the hotel manager to get us food. A sumptuous dinner of lamb biryani and chicken qorma with tandoori naan appeased our appetites. Over dinner we agreed unanimously that if we ever needed another profession, it would be pelt smuggling because it was so easy to do. But to be fair to the authorities, finding one pelt or trophy is like looking for a needle in a haystack. The experience brought home to me the fact that the illegal trade in wildlife will never be stopped through surveillance in countries that lack the resources and the means to carry out that surveillance effectively. In such places, conservation policies must address the root causes of the illegal trade.

The next morning we drove to the Pakistan Natural History Museum. The director, who was expecting us, greeted us warmly and showed his eagerness to see the pelt. His eyes lit up as I spread it out on his office floor. "It's in very good shape," he said happily. "This will be an excellent addition to the exhibit." He told us it would be about a month or so before the pelt would be ready for display and asked if we would like our names mentioned as donors on a plaque. We requested that it be left anonymous. After tea and a tour of the museum, we left, lighthearted and relaxed without the burden of the pelt.

ALI ABUTALIP DAHASHOF

TWO SNOW LEOPARDS, MY FATHER, AND ME

(TRANSLATED FROM CHINESE BY RICH HARRIS)

CHINA—*Much can change in a generation. A son admires his father's heroic deed but finds a different path for himself.*

Whenever people talk about snow leopards, I can't help but think back to my childhood, to the story of my father and the two snow leopards he killed with his bare hands.

My father, Abutalip Dahashof, was born into a Kazak family in 1913 in the high Altai Mountain region near the place where the borders of Mongolia, Kazakhstan, and China come together. By today's standards, his family of nine lived simply and was poor. During the late 1920s the local people who lived in the Altai region of Xinjiang engaged in resistance against nationalist forces. One day in 1926 a bomb exploded in the doorway of my father's family's house, killing everyone except my father and uncle. At thirteen and four, respectively, they had no choice but to begin a wandering life, making do for their livelihoods as best they could. Many Kazak families migrated westward, some as far as India, Pakistan, and Turkey. My father and uncle, however, traveled eastward to Gansu Province, where they learned to herd livestock for a meager living. Through the kind introduction of others, my father met and married my mother. But the three were so poor that they could claim but a single sheepskin and a woolen rug as possessions.

Under the newly established People's Republic of China, some Kazaks in Gansu settled near two large lakes, Suhai Nor and Bulunyn Nor, near the border with Qinghai and Xinjiang. The new government provided most families with livestock to help them start herds. My father and others were given about fifty sheep, as well as a few cattle and camels. He settled in the Bulunyn Nor area (Aksai Autonomous Kazakh County), and within a few years his herd had increased more than fourfold. Life remained difficult for my father and others like him. On the edge of the beautiful but harsh Qinghai-Tibetan Plateau, little precipitation and cold climate slowed vegetation growth. Summers barely warmed, and winter temperatures typically reached minus 34 degrees Fahrenheit.

One particularly cold winter day my father had gotten up early, mounted his horse, and driven the sheep herd to the grassland pastures. The sheep suddenly stopped and refused to move any further. My father quickly rode to see what had frightened them. Almost immediately he encountered something hiding in the tall grass but was unable to make out exactly what it was. Then my father thought, "Ah, surely this is a wolf that has come to eat some of my sheep." His first thought was wolf because the grazing area was a plateau marsh with no mountains, cliffs, or talus rocks— the natural habitat for snow leopards. He never considered that the sheep might be fearful of a large cat. He dismounted and approached cautiously. To his amazement, he found not one but two snow leopards.

His sheep dog began to chase the two cats along the adjacent lakeshore, barking furiously all the while, with my father in close pursuit on horseback. The snow leopards eventually stopped running and turned toward the dog, glaring and baring their teeth. Seeing that this situation could end badly for his dog, my father whipped his horse into a gallop and quickly caught up to the animals engaged in the standoff. From his horse he managed to grab the long tail of one of the snow leopards from behind and began beating its head with his leather whip in the other hand until it was no longer breathing. The second snow leopard, sensing that its life was in peril, fled the scene. It ran along the other bank of the lake with the sheep dog in hot pursuit, followed by my father charging on his horse at full gallop. Like most Kazak, he was an expert horseman. The dog put the cat into a position from which it could neither escape nor turn to parry the attack. Again from horseback, my father seized the snow leopard's tail and beat the animal with his whip. His young, strong arms quickly brought death to the second snow leopard.

That afternoon my father packed the dead snow leopards on his horse, rounded up the sheep herd, and headed back to our ger (the typical circular home of nomads throughout Asia's high steppe). The other herdsmen in camp were surprised to see the snow leopards; most of them didn't know they existed in the area. Everyone in camp was impressed that my father had slain them with his bare hands.

The story of his deed spread like prairie fire throughout neighboring villages. Herdsmen gathered to praise my father as a snow leopard–hunting hero. By killing the snow leopards, he had not only protected his sheep but those of his neighbors as well. For herding families, any loss of livestock cut deeply into their already marginal existence. In appreciation and admiration, they named my father the local pastoralist leader. Ironically, those two snow leopards were the only wildlife my father killed in his entire life.

I remember as a child the cold winter days when my mother would rise early in the frozen dawn and put on her coat made from the luxuriant pelts of the snow leopards. Cuddled in her arms, I had no idea I owed my warmth to two wild snow leopards.

My early childhood and teenage years were spent on the high grasslands. When I was old enough I went to school in town, returning to the grasslands during vacations to help my family tend livestock. My mother's snow leopard coat always hung at a prominent place in our ger. In school, we read a lesson about snow leopards, but I still didn't know of their connection to my family. One summer I asked my mother about her coat and heard for the first time about my father's heroic exploit. On vacations from school, I would spend time with my father, observing and learning about local wildlife as we tended our herds. Though renowned for killing two snow leopards, my father taught me to value and respect wildlife. He died in 1993, but his life lessons and his stories live on in my memory.

Years passed, and I eventually went to high school in Beijing and to college in Lanzhou, earning a degree in agricultural studies. I later joined the staff at our small community's wildlife protection station, where I learned more about wildlife and gained an appreciation for all of earth's creatures. In the spring of 1999 a local herdsman found a young, emaciated snow leopard that had apparently been abandoned by its mother. The herdsman had taken the cub home, where he fed it wild hare and food scraps. Dr. Rich Harris, my colleague on an argali study, and I arranged to see the cub at the herdsman's home. Dr. Harris had the proper equipment to immobilize the cub so we could safely weigh and examine it. With the herdsman's blessing, we loaded the drugged cat into the back seat of our battered old jeep and drove far into the mountains. We released it at a site we knew would not have livestock for months and had abundant natural prey. I don't know if this small snow leopard lived, but at least it was given a second chance. Decades after my father's encounter, I finally got to see a wild snow leopard up close. On this day, Ali, son of Dahash, used his strength and wisdom to save the life of a snow leopard.

A few years later I was fortunate to have a second encounter with a snow leopard. It happened while I was guiding foreign hunters at the Kharteng International Hunting Area in my home of Aksai County. One autumn day while riding my horse, I happened upon an adult snow leopard eating a fresh kill. It was feeding on a horse that looked to be about two years old. Before I knew it, my horse had taken me very close to the big cat. Too close, really, and it was broad daylight. Fortunately, I eased my horse away from the scene without incident. Astride my horse, I thought of my father's encounter and could not imagine actually reaching down and grabbing hold of the animal's tail—truly, his was a remarkable feat of courage, strength, and horsemanship.

In 2008, at a conference in Beijing, I had the good fortune to meet many of the world's leading snow leopard researchers. From the lectures and interaction with the experts at the conference, I expanded my knowledge and understanding of snow leopard ecology. I've developed a deep bond with snow leopards. From my research I've had the opportunity to note specific behaviors of the cats in my region, including opportunistic hunting in the daylight hours. I've noticed also that, since 1980, increased human activity and more intensified agricultural production have gradually reduced the distribution of snow leopards in Gansu Province. Snow leopards have likely disappeared from the southern and eastern portions of the province.

Fortunately, the big mountain ranges of western Gansu still harbor large numbers of blue sheep, argali, and other potential prey species for the snow leopard. The snow leopard and its prey prefer very rough topography, generally above 13,000 feet, which keeps human activity low in these ranges. During recent years, when we surveyed flora and fauna, we often observed fresh snow leopard footprints, droppings, and fresh kills of wild sheep. Occasionally, we came across livestock killed by snow leopards. At these sites I thought of the loss to a herding family barely getting by. I also thought of my father, overcoming fear, killing two snow leopards with his hands to protect his precious few livestock. I am glad snow leopards have not disappeared from my homeland. Though it will never be easy, I will work hard to find ways for herder and snow leopard to coexist. In my heart, I believe my father would approve.

E V G E N I Y P. K A S H K A R O V

HAPPY DAYS

KYRGYZSTAN—*The author recounts incredible up-close encounters with two snow leopards that become a salubrious memory.*

As a kid growing up in Novokuznetsk, Siberia, whenever I got sick my mother would tell me that if I concentrated on the happy days of my life, good health would return more quickly. As an adult, I enjoy good health most of the time, but when I do get sick I fall back on my mother's remedy of long ago. If I were to get sick today, my thoughts would turn to two remarkably happy days in the Tien Shan Mountains of Kirgizia. Just thinking about those days as I write this brings a smile to my face and lightens my heart.

Each winter for more than a decade I would take a field expedition into the heart of this range, which lies north and west of the Taklamakan Desert and borders Kazakhstan, Kyrgyzstan, and China's Xinjiang Autonomous Region. As a scientist with the Academy of Science of Kirgizia, my job was to monitor the "key area" — about 1,000 square miles of the central Tien Shan, a unique region that represents the three distinct biogeographical zones of the entire range and exemplifies the diverse habitat of the charismatic snow leopard (*irbis* in Mongolian and Russian).

The northern key area resembles Siberia—marginal snow leopard habitat. The middle key area is habitat for bighorn sheep such as argali and looks similar to the Eastern Pamir Plateau and the Tibetan Plateau—poor snow leopard habitat. Finally, the inner key area—especially the Sarychat-Irtash-Uchkul River basin, with abundant grazing for wintering domestic livestock and habitat for ibex and mountain sheep—constitutes good snow leopard habitat. From our surveys, we found that densities of snow leopard and its prey were higher here than in any other region of the Tien Shan.

There was no easy way to get to my study area in the central Tien Shan. My choices were to ski four to five days, crossing a 13,700-foot pass; or to take two to three days riding with geologists who worked a gold mine, camping in small villages, then skiing the last 18½ miles. Everything I needed to sustain me in the field had to be carried in on my backpack, which never weighed less than about 80 pounds. A second route ran through less mountainous relief, something between tundra and steppe, allowing me to use a sledge for the final part of the trip. Early in the project, I had to build a small cabin for shelter against the snow and as a base camp for longer sojourns farther into the mountains. The cabin made it possible to work in the winter, when temperatures bottomed at minus 58 degrees Fahrenheit. I spent forty-two days taking apart a dilapidated old herder's house and reconstructing a new shelter at a sunnier location about 1,600 feet away. I arranged the windows so I could easily scan the nearby river terraces and ridges. Basic comforts included a long table, two plank beds, and a cast-iron stove. Though the shelter could accommodate four, most of the time it was just me.

The first happy day: in December 1986 my good friend and colleague Victor Mishenin and I conducted a wildlife survey along the Koilyu River. The river forked; Victor took the north fork, I took the south. As night closed, I headed back to camp a few miles downriver. Nearing the camp, I could make out my footprints left earlier in the day, but intercrossed with my tracks were those of three snow leopards. They tracked back and forth from one slope to the other. Raising my head from the tracks, I spotted an adult male and female lying on a big flat stone not more than 300 feet above me. They looked at me with curiosity but not alarm. I froze immediately, not wanting to frighten them and awestruck by this rare encounter. For the next few minutes we gazed at each other, man and animal locked in mutual fascination. I had no zoom lens for my old Russian-made camera, so I tried a shot through the lens of my binoculars. It turned out better than expected and was eventually published. With darkness settling fast, I rushed to camp to tell Victor of my good fortune. We hurried to the big stone, finding both cats resting side by side as before. The next day we found prints of the sub-adult "teenager" near the big stone. It appeared that the three of them were hunting ibex.

Snow leopards, owners of wilderness, seldom grant such casual meetings with humans. We were guests in their home, a home without doors and windows. Thanks to them, we felt much closer to Mother Nature. The coming night over the Tien Shan was peaceful, unveiling an unforgettable starry sky. Around a glowing campfire, Victor and I pondered our gift of happiness and hoped for a day when people and wildlife can find common language and live together without hunting or cruelty.

My second happy day: four years later, also in December, in Tien Shan, and with Victor. This time we were about 30 miles lower down the river at Bashkul Lake, 11,500 feet above sea level. Above all others, Bashkul is my favorite place in Tien Shan because I believe my soul lives there. In early winter, a layer of ice blankets Bashkul. All day and night the lake emits eerie creaks and groans like an old, tired warrior sighing beneath the ice. Bashkul's water and ice are incredibly clear. Walking along the shoreline, I've seen many ibex and sheep horns under the ice, a telling of wolf kills the previous winter. The area, only small squares of pasture scattered among rock fields, isn't well suited for domestic stock. But ibex and mountain sheep thrive in this landscape, thus so do snow leopards. Fearing the loss of valuable livestock, some herdsmen set traps for snow leopards. On this trip we made the acquaintance of a herdsman named Karnauchy (which translates as "broken ear"). Though a little suspicious, Karnauchy, like all Kirgiz, was genuinely hospitable to Victor and me, sharing tea in the warmth of his yurt.

On the shortest day of the year, we spent a few hours at Bashkul Lake surveying for ibex and signs of snow leopard. On the trails used by snow leopard we found seven or eight large traps. We broke them and hid the pieces under rocks. Even though the herdsmen were kind to us, we could not abide their efforts to trap and kill snow leopards. Just as we were about to turn in for the night, Victor and I decided to check one more trail near camp. Early on the path we noticed fresh pugmarks, snow leopard tracks. But something seemed wrong; the path also showed signs of something dragging alongside the tracks. We concluded it was a snow leopard in a trap, dragging the log meant to keep it from leaving the trap site. From the freshness of the sign, it seemed to be just ahead of us.

There was no time for us to think about what to do because darkness was coming quickly. We had maybe twenty to thirty minutes of light to find the trapped cat. Our thoughts switched between the consequences of not finding the cat before nightfall and finding a large predator in the night. With binoculars we spotted our quarry near a juniper bush about 225 feet up the canyon. As best we could tell, it looked to be a young adult male, maybe two or three years old. A clawed spring trap was firmly clamped on his left front paw and tangled around the juniper.

Knowing we had little time before dark, our choice was simple: Victor would pull on the snow leopard's tail while I pulled on the front paw, releasing the trap. I knew the difficult part was to release the trap, an exercise that usually calls for two legs bearing down on the trap to release the pressure. But I couldn't position myself to open the trap with both legs; a snarling snow leopard swiping at my legs made it impossible. Desperate, I knew what I had to do—I would have to pull the clamped leg as far away as possible from the free leg to keep it from lacerating my arm. On the count of "one, two, three," Victor pulled the tail taut while I pulled the trapped leg, opening the jaws of the trap with strength that comes only when fueled by massive quantities of adrenaline. I managed to free the leg. Victor feared that the freed snow leopard would immediately turn and swipe at him; I feared that, once released, it would swipe at me. Luckily, we both were wrong. The freed leopard barely moved when it was released from the trap. Perhaps traumatized by the whole event, it simply didn't move. We threw small stones at it to make sure it cleared the area. We did not want Karnauchy to find it the next day. It finally moved out, limping but at least moving away. It made it to the canyon wall, falling backward but finally making it to the ridgeline.

It snowed that night, lightly rustling on our tent. Early the next morning the snow leopard was gone, free to resume what we hoped would be a long life. Victor and I once again counted our blessings that we were in the right place at the right time.

Nineteen years later, while on a survey in a sheep-hunting reserve near the China border, I noticed one of the rangers looking at me suspiciously. It was Karnauchy, only now, in addition to a broken ear, he sported a broken nose as well. Older and with much longer hair, he wasn't sure about me. He will never know that Victor and I released a prize from his trap one cold December night.

Karnauchy and others like him continue to slaughter snow leopards. Black markets in all countries from Altai to Himalaya are well supplied with snow leopard skins. In 1995, during the celebration of the 1,000-year anniversary of the People's Age of Manas in Kirgizia, regional exhibitions displayed close to 200 poached snow leopard pelts. It will take the weight of government and influential conservation organizations for Karnauchy and others to give up the practice of killing snow leopards. Although poaching continues, many successful research projects have improved our understanding of the snow leopards' situation. Even though great new photos and exciting films also have not stopped poaching, they have increased awareness and broadened support. In 1947 Maxim Zverev was the first person to photograph a snow leopard in the wild. In the sixty-five years hence, two generations have joined the greater cause to protect snow leopards, leading to the creation of the Snow Leopard Network (SLN), a union of professionals dedicated to snow leopard conservation. Thanks to the SLN, we see photos taken in Pakistan, India, Nepal, Kazakhstan, Russia, and Mongolia, confirming that snow leopard populations still survive throughout their range. They trust us, trust our help, and demonstrate friendly relationships for collaboration.

One day I will probably be sick, but I will not be afraid because I have a medicine. My medicine is the remembrance of two happy days with snow leopards, when Victor and I observed these big cats for a few hours and had the exceptionally rare privilege to hold one, to feel of one blood for a moment.

NASIER A. KITCHLOO

RAISING SHERU

INDIA—*Faced with a difficult choice, a wildlife warden chooses to raise a young snow leopard.*

From my study, the knock at my door sounded faint, tentative. Usually, those who come to my home after office hours are disturbed—angry about foreign tourists not paying their bills, marauding wolves killing livestock, or crop-raiding shapo or kiang (the endemic wild sheep and wild ass). As wildlife warden for Ladakh, an area slightly smaller than Scotland, I was accustomed to after-hour visits from locals with wildlife problems and those who wanted to talk about the conservation of Ladakh's unique wildlife heritage. Assigned to Leh from Srinagar, I tried to maintain an open business and personal environment, sensitive to being a non-local and a Muslim in India's largest enclave of Tibetan Buddhists.

Padma, my assistant, personal secretary, and housekeeper, bolted into the study. "Come quickly, Nasier Saab" he said. The old woman at my door looked tired and worried. "*Sheru, sheru*" (Urdu for big cat) she said in an excited, desperate tone, holding up her dilapidated basket so I could see the contents. Swaddled inside were two baby snow leopards, both sound asleep. I invited her in and asked Padma to make tea. All important matters in Ladakh begin and end with tea. Slowly, the old one began to relax and let her story unfold. She was from Hinachey, a small village in the Nubra Valley about 75 miles north of Leh. To reach Leh, she had journeyed all day on a crowded bus made worse by August heat and a winding road that climbs up and then down Khardung La, at over 17,500 feet India's highest motorable pass. She had found the two cubs near the family dwelling, the traditional yak hair tent of nomadic herding families. The barking of two small camp dogs had caught her attention. She went to investigate, finding the cubs huddled together, hissing at the young dogs. She found no evidence of the mother, and later that evening she asked the family if anyone had seen any evidence of a snow leopard while shepherding. No one had. That night, after considerable discussion, the family decided that the cubs should be brought to me, the chief caretaker of Ladakh's wildlife. As Buddhists, they could not abide to let the cubs perish in the wild.

The old woman told her story and then looked to me for an answer, for relief. Her sad eyes and steady speech betrayed no subversion in her explanation; she appeared genuinely distressed over the young cubs' well-being. Over the years I had learned to take care in such cases, as it is not uncommon for herders to kill snow leopards in retaliation for the animals having killed their livestock. For some, it comes down to basic survival — even Buddhists have limits to the degree of loss they can tolerate from predators. Livestock loss can devastate poor families barely eking out a living in the high pastures. And snow leopards are efficient killers, especially of penned animals. I personally attended to an incident where a single snow leopard had attacked forty-five sheep and goats from a herd of seventy-five. About half were killed, suffocated by bites to the windpipe; the others were exhausted from fright. Snow leopards have been known to kill over a hundred animals in a single night, a killing-frenzy behavior that continues to baffle the experts. Much of my time was spent trying to find ways to reduce such encounters between the snow leopard and the people who share its world. But this old woman presented me with a vastly different situation. Two wild snow leopard cubs were suddenly in need of human care—my care—to survive.

I received my education in wildlife management from one of India's finest colleges and studied abroad on several occasions, granting me a unique perspective on my profession from both Eastern and Western viewpoints. Yet all my training failed me when faced with the penetrating eyes of this gentle woman. She looked to me as the protector, the arbiter of wisdom in all matters wildlife. I could sense her uneasiness, her fear that I may not share her sensibilities toward wild things, living things. My Western training would have me view parks and protected areas as mostly free of people and managed so that nature can be nature. Under such management the cubs should have been left to die. In contrast, India's hundreds of parks and protected areas include few that do not have local people living in them.

In Ladakh I oversee the Karakorum and Changtang Sanctuaries and Hemis National Park, over 8,000 square miles of mountains and high plateau. Inside these reserves, hundreds of families live alongside rare wildlife such as chiru (Tibetan antelope), nayan (argali), kiang, wild yak, and black-necked crane. Ladakh, the "land of high passes," possesses a stark mountain beauty found nowhere else on earth. Beneath the beauty, however, is a harsh world for those who live among the great mountain ranges of the Himalaya and Karakorum and on the Tibetan Plateau, where the average elevation is over 14,700 feet, sometimes called the "roof of the world." Although they don't have to do so, through a unique connection of faith the Ladakhi people choose to coexist with wildlife. The Buddhist family that found these cubs abhors any death of their livestock to snow leopards, yet they could not abandon two sentient lives—the cubs could not be left to die. They could have eliminated two future night stalkers, but instead they chose life and the added burden of a long-distance journey. Denning, or the killing of young wolf and coyote pups, is a common practice in some Western cultures. Within me the battle raged: "I should not encourage such wildlife rescues, no matter how benevolent, for they seldom turn out well," said one side of my brain. I've read and seen the heartwarming movies of human-grown African lions joyously returned back into the wild, but no one has ever raised snow leopards and then reintroduced them into the wild. Such a feat would be impossible in the snow leopards' near-vertical world and with prey that thrive in the most rugged terrain imaginable. Other than a quick death, the best outcome would be a caged life, forever imprisoned, never knowing or experiencing the freedom to roam the far pavilions visible from behind bars. What was I to do?

The small cubs awoke and began to stir. They appeared to be only a couple of weeks old and clearly in a weakened state. Curled together, eyes not fully opened, they were pure kitty cuteness. My science brain chastised my emotional brain for thinking of such an unprofessional term. I gave the old woman my assessment of the situation, issuing a small prayer that I wouldn't regret what I was about to tell her.

"*Amma Lay*, you have done a good thing," I said, using the respectful salutation for elder women. "Go home now and know that I will care for these young ones as my own children" — words from the other side of my brain. Her eyes immediately brightened, and the broad grin across her wrinkled face brought a smile to my own. Her hands cupped around mine, she bowed repeatedly, backing out my front door uttering "*ya joo, ya joo, ya joo*" (Ladakhi for thank you). She promised that Buddha would take note of such kindness and repay me many-fold in this life or the next.

Padma looked at the cubs, then looked at me with a quizzical expression. It took a few seconds for me to clear my mind of the clutter of indecision and focus on what to do. "Padma," I said, "we have become parents." A smile widened his face. I sent him into town to find fresh milk and ask advice from anyone familiar with raising kittens. I settled the cubs in my study.

Padma returned from the local market with cow's milk and formula given by an elder he knew in Leh. She said to water down the milk before giving it to the cubs. She shared other helpful hints on how to get them interested in feeding. It worked. The cubs fed, one more than the other. Padma and I became wet-nurses to little balls of fur, each of us holding vigil when the other was out.

Sadly, after two days one of the cubs died, despite our best efforts. We doubled our effort and attention on the remaining cub until it picked up a routine of feeding and playing, repeated around the clock. It was heartening to see it gain strength and romp around my study. Padma became the consummate father, tending to the needs of Sheru, our name for the little one.

Sheru came to us in late August 1997. By winter she had grown in size, strength, and playfulness. By spring she began to find new ways to expend her pent-up, youthful energy. Often, I would come home to find another set of curtains shredded, a shoe gnawed beyond recognition, rugs tattered, and claw marks on furniture. With the onset of warmer weather we enclosed the porch and moved Sheru outside. From the moment her eyes first opened, she and I routinely locked eyes as though we were talking through the portals of our souls. Her large, round feline eyes shone brilliant, clear, and all-seeing. I sensed an incarnate intelligence beyond a mere wild cat.

From the beginning, Sheru's diet was a problem. Fresh milk was easier to get than fresh meat products, especially in winter when Leh becomes a ghost town compared with its summer contingent of tourists from around the world. In winter, virtually everything is flown in daily from Delhi or weekly from Chandigarh, Jammu, and Srinagar. My department tolerated my raising Sheru but provided no stipend for food or care. All expenses came from my own pocket. Winters were also hard on me, separated from my family. My wife was a physician in Srinagar and also cared for our two children, Shehriyar and Abrar. Once the high pass between Srinagar and Leh closed after the first snows, I was separated from my family for the winter. Even in nice weather it was a two-day mountainous journey. Sheru was a welcome distraction from the monotony of winter when, because of poor roads and extreme cold (down to minus 22 degrees Fahrenheit), I traveled less to the parks and sanctuaries. She was always excited to see Padma and me, leaping and spinning and swiping with glee at our arrival.

By summer, approaching a year old, Sheru had grown and gained weight. It became clear she needed a larger place to live, and I had the solution. I had built a pen for captive-breeding chiru, a native antelope species of the high Tibetan Plateau. These hardy ungulates grow what is arguably the finest wool in the world, known locally as *shahtoosh*. For centuries, the men and women of Kashmir have woven shahtoosh into shawls of the finest quality, often as wedding gifts known as "ring shawls," woven so fine they can easily pass through a wedding ring. Chiru numbers had fallen from the millions at the turn of the twentieth century to fewer than 75,000. At the time, my department wanted to evaluate the option of captive-breeding cheru under the assumption that if captive animals could produce legal shahtoosh, the illegal trade would disappear. The project was stalled by red tape and sorting out how to safely capture cheru in their remote habitat, which borders Aksai Chin, an area under Chinese control. Thus the newly built enclosure had no immediate use, so it became Sheru's new home, replete with swinging tires—which she loved—boulders, and other structures that allowed her to stalk, sprint, and spring about all day. The structure was located next to my residence. Sheru adjusted to our daily routine, and no matter what the time, she came to life whenever Padma or I arrived home. No doubt, she brought joy to my life for I, too, enjoyed coming home to play with her, communing through our eyes.

My residence was only a five-minute drive from the Leh airport, a hub for tourists but also home to one of India's largest military bases. All day huge military transport planes would fly in and out, filling our peaceful world with the sounds of human-made thunder. We adjusted to the gigantic metal birds coming and going.

Sheru soon became a well-known local attraction. Locals came with their families, sometimes spending hours admiring Sheru. I would serve tea on these occasions, enjoying the company of the townspeople. I'm convinced that these gatherings, centered on Sheru, helped to ingratiate me with Leh's populace. Military families, filmmakers, biologists, and tourists from around the world came for a close-up look at a real snow leopard, the mythical big cat of the surrounding mountains that so few see in the wild. We even had visits from high-level dignitaries from the US Consulate and the Indian government. Most amazed of all were the herding families that came down out of the mountains. In Buddhist culture two animals bring good fortune when seen: black-necked crane and snow leopard. Sheru's presence was a blessing to Leh locals and to the poor villagers who rarely come to town. Many enjoyable hours were passed having tea with visitors as Sheru romped and played.

I arranged my house so I could see Sheru's pen from every room. She never failed to jump with excitement whenever Padma or I came around, wanting a pat on the head and recognition just like a young kid. I struggled mightily with a deep desire to let her run and romp outside the cage. The cage meant life for her, but I remained conflicted about denying her a wild life, a chance to run free, jump, play, and stretch her lithe body on the steep mountains she saw from her enclosure. Often, I felt her eyes were saying, "Let me out for awhile, just let me run for a few hours and I will come right back." When he learned about my internal struggle, Padma took control of the keys so I would not enter her cage or feel tempted to set her free. I considered trying to find Sheru a mate, but that would have been difficult, and some felt that keeping Sheru caged was not a good thing.

Unlike the residents of Leh, who largely hibernate in winter, Sheru loved winter temperatures. Summers were the opposite for her. Slowly over several months, I began to see in Sheru's eyes something new, something troubling that I didn't understand but could feel. At this same time, my life and career became less settled: after seven years in Leh it was time to consider a career move, perhaps closer to my family. My father fell ill with cancer, which helped me decide to take a new post in Srinagar where I could be closer to him and my family. But what was I to do with Sheru? I couldn't bear the thought of leaving her behind, but I knew she could not accompany me to all future postings, no matter how much I might welcome her.

Kismet means destiny in Urdu. At this critical juncture in both Sheru's and my lives, I received an inquiry from the Padmaja Naidu Himalayan Zoological Park in Darjeeling (PNHZP), a reputable endangered species breeding center. They had heard about

Sheru and were interested in her as a breeding cat, since she came from the wild and had wild genes. Suddenly, things began to come together. A California-based nongovernmental organization joined with the PNHZP to arrange aerial transportation for Sheru. I rationalized that this was the best possible option for Sheru, the optimum destiny for a human-raised snow leopard. She needed a secure, long-term home. At the PNHZP she would receive great care, live among other snow leopards, and have the opportunity to pass along her genes, thereby reinvigorating snow leopards in zoos. In 2000 Sheru was flown to the PNHZP; I took a new post in Srinagar and resumed my life with my family.

After some time I lost track of Sheru, choosing not to visit her in Darjeeling. Part of me wanted to make it a clean break, remembering her only as we lived together in Leh. Part of me did not want to look into her eyes again, sensing her longing to romp free of the cage, reigniting a longing in me to set her free. Through friends, I heard that she was all right, but I never knew the details of her time at the PNHZP. It was rumored that a snow leopard taken from the wild about the same time as Sheru had died. I was never contacted, so I presumed it was not Sheru. When I was writing this story, I needed to know with certainty what had happened to Sheru. The answer wasn't immediate because there was confusion about the cats, but finally the director of the PNHZP confirmed that Sheru is still alive. When she arrived at the PNHZP she was renamed Neeta. Now thirteen years old, she is the grand dame of the center, having had her fourth set of cubs—triplets—in 2009. Sheru/Neeta may not have led a life in the wild, but she has lived as long as wild snow leopards, and she contributed her genes to several generations so that captive cats might enjoy the genetic vigor that comes only from wild genes. I'm comforted in knowing that the young kitten I raised a decade ago still lives—even if an enclosed life. Her transformative eyes still live in my soul, as do the gentle eyes of the old woman who helped me make the choice to raise Sheru.

I'm often asked what I would do if faced with the same situation again. I know what I would do. What would you do?

TOM McCARTHY

CUBS

MONGOLIA, KYRGYZSTAN—*A noted snow leopard scientist and father describes two young cubs that capture his heart.*

For nearly two decades I have been exceedingly privileged to have been able to make a living doing something most people can only dream of—studying snow leopards. And yes, I am one of the fortunate few, even among my peers, who has seen a wild snow leopard in its native habitat, several in fact. Not that it could ever become mundane, gazing at a beast so mythically rare and elusive. Had I seen fifty in the wild, and the actual number is not even half that, each encounter would still be as inspiring as my first. A moment with a snow leopard on its home ground, playing by its rules, is an ethereal and moving occurrence that is not soon forgotten. So when asked if I could write about some of my most profound or heart-touching experiences in the presence of snow leopards, I had to sort through a fair number of emotion-filled memories to settle on a couple that I wanted to share. In the end, it was a fairly easy decision and it came down to tales of cubs, all now grown but just cubs at the time and the source of some of my most personally inspiring recollections.

My first cub tale took place not long after I first started studying snow leopards. Mind you, that was before the age of Global Positioning System (GPS) collars that transmit precise locations via satellite to researchers back in camp or even sitting comfortably in a remote office. My study, like the very few previous studies of snow leopards, relied on simple very high frequency (VHF) collars that sent out a radio "ping" picked up by a handheld receiver and directional antenna. The rest is leg work as you get a bearing on the cat's location from a number of different angles until you can estimate pretty accurately where it is—all the while traipsing through some of the highest, most rugged, unforgiving terrain on the planet, in temperatures ranging from minus 35 to 110 degrees Fahrenheit. I don't mean to get off on a "back in my day . . ." rant here; I'm just adding perspective on what snow leopard research was like at the time. Besides, since I am now one of those researchers sitting in a comfy office in the United States watching the snow leopard GPS data pour in via satellite, I know the value of both the high-tech and low-tech study methods. It was definitely the low-tech method that gave me my fist cub experience.

Three years into my PhD research in southwestern Mongolia, I had managed to capture five snow leopards: two males and three females. Following them through the mountains and valleys of my 250-square-mile study had proved a daunting task, and it was not unusual for any one cat to disappear on me for two or three months at a time. They could simply get around in that terrain a lot better and faster than I could, and, once I lost them, finding them again was next to impossible. Unless they decided to wander back close to my base camp and we could start the game afresh. Because my goal was to collect as many locations for each cat as possible and thus gain an understanding of their habitat use and needs, I didn't really need to observe the cats after I radio-collared them and sent them on their way. I just needed to use that radio "ping" to determine their location and record it. Yet no matter how scientifically focused my study, these were snow leopards, and I wanted to get a glimpse of them now and then. But that was a rarity that, up until the third year of my study, I could count on one hand, despite months and months of arduous daily tracking. Elusive things, snow leopards. Summer of the third year was to bring a change in luck.

The last cat I collared during the study was a beautiful young female. We were very fortunate to have met her, since she almost slipped by us on the winter day we ended up catching her. Later that summer, after a brief hiatus, I returned to base camp with my young Mongolian project biologist to resume tracking our cats for one final year. As was often the case, we found a few of our cats close to camp, an area with abundant ibex, the scimitar-horned wild goats that constitute the mainstay of a snow leopard's diet in this part of their range. We spent the first week or so tracking our biggest male, since he seemed to get incredible joy out of allowing us to find him once or twice before heading off to some remote corner of his home range for a month. So focusing on him was a priority when he was near, even though we could hear the pings from our young female from somewhere not far off. More of a short-range traveler and easier to keep up with, she could wait. But when the big male finally did his normal Houdini act and left us with nothing but silence in our radio headsets, we turned our attention to our young lady.

We knew she was somewhere up a long wide valley that ran north from base camp, so we started out early with tracking gear, lunch, cameras, and a spotting scope. It was a running joke in camp that if we took a camera or the spotting scope, we were assured of nothing to see or photograph, so we assumed that at best we would get a good fix on her position and build stamina by carrying all that gear into the mountains for nothing. As we followed the signal up the gently sloping valley, her radio signal indicated she was actually somewhere high up a steep ridge running off to one side. Of course. Tempting as it was to leave all but the radio gear behind, we shrugged and scaled the rock and scree cliff with full packs, topping out 1,500 feet above the valley floor. Crawling cautiously over the final outcrop, we found ourselves at the top end of a side canyon and the ping of the leopard's radio collar booming in the headset. She was close! The signal was coming from somewhere below us in the side canyon. A large boulder gave us just enough cover to glass the canyon with our binoculars, but nothing stirred and the radio ping stayed loud and seemed stationary. Moving with caution and trying to stay within the small area of cover the boulder provided, we set up tripods for the spotting scope and camera. Were we going to break the jinx and actually see something? Not soon, it turned out. For nearly two hours we stared through the spotting scope and binoculars at the brushy patch 200 yards below us that seemed the source of the signal. Only the grass below us blew in the wind, while the ping from the collar taunted. We ate lunch.

Then, with no detectable movement, almost as if she had been poised in full view the entire time, our girl was out of the brush and standing broadside to us. What little movement we had been making ceased—we barely breathed. But after several minutes we could sense that her attention was not directed up the canyon toward us but back into the brush. Something there held her gaze, yet it didn't seem to be food or a threat; her posture said otherwise. Before my mental wheels could turn fast enough to make a guess as to what was in the thicket, a ball of fur came bursting out, landing at the female's feet. And then another and another. Cubs! Three of them!

Oblivious to anything other than mom and their siblings, the two-month-olds tussled with each other and rolled across the dusty canyon floor, bouncing off their mother's legs and rocks with total abandon, finally crashing into a shallow ravine. Clearly, snow leopards learn their stealth as they grow rather than being born into it. The female moved slowly toward them, then stopped and froze. Through the spotting scope I could see the hairs on her neck stand up, and then she slowly turned toward us. Even at 200 yards I swear she was looking directly into my eyes through my spotting scope. She was not pleased. Moving swiftly, she dropped into the ravine and pushed the cubs up the opposite side, then hurried past them, heading for the far side of the canyon. Two cubs followed, but the third had found something interesting to bat at. Mom was having none of it and raced back, grasping the oblivious straggler in her mouth and trotting toward the canyon wall, which she scaled in two or three easy bounds. The other two cubs were not so skilled and struggled to make the top, sliding back a foot for each two steps forward until mom came back and nudged them up and over. Once they had all made the canyon rim, our girl stopped and looked back at us. One cub glanced our way, seemingly wondering what all the fuss was about. Then the entire family dropped out of sight and was gone.

The whole affair lasted barely five minutes, yet it brought elation and awe that have not diminished as I reflect back on that day fourteen years later. The energy of the cubs alongside the defiant determination of the mother sent a simple but clear message: "Left to ourselves we will be fine." The long hike back to camp that day seemed a lot easier for a change. The dust, sweat, hunger, cold, and exhaustion of the job fell away; and a sense of optimism for these four cats and their kind settled in. It was a good feeling. I never saw those cubs again, despite months of tracking. That snow leopard mother learned well and always kept her charges well hidden, denying us a second peek. But once was enough.

My second cub tale took place a decade later and a thousand miles away in the central Asian state of Kyrgyzstan. Historically, most snow leopards brought out of the wild for the world's zoos came from this relatively small country, which boasted a very large snow leopard population. By the mid-1990s — suffering extreme economic hardship in the period immediately after the collapse of the Soviet Union, of which it was part — the country's snow leopards were being decimated by illegal trade in pelts, bones, and live cats. Often, the instigators were the wildlife guards who had previously protected the cats but now had no other way to feed their families. Or by corrupt government officials who saw a lucrative way to further line their own pockets at the expense of one more plundered national treasure. It was in that daunting scenario that we started a snow leopard research and conservation program in 2002, with a model program focused on a key snow leopard reserve, Sarychat Ertash, in the central Tien Shan Mountains. A community-based conservation approach that had been very successful elsewhere was replicated in and near the reserve. Local people benefited from improved livelihoods as the result of a handicraft development project, and in exchange they agreed to not kill snow leopards or allow poachers into the Sarychat Ertash Reserve. After a few years the program appeared to be making a difference, at least in terms of local people's income and awareness of snow leopard conservation issues. But what about the cats? Were they rebounding from near extirpation at the hands of poachers and traders experienced in the late 1990s?

There are very few ways to determine the status of an animal as elusive and cryptic as the snow leopard. You don't just walk out into the mountains and count them. But by 2005 a handful of new technologies were available that held promise in monitoring cat numbers, such as noninvasive genetics and remote automated cameras. Sarychat Ertash, a place where we needed to know how well our conservation efforts were working, was a potential proving ground for both. All we needed were some willing researchers to spend the necessary time in the remote core of the high-altitude reserve to complete such a study. I knew of a couple of candidates.

By the time I started my PhD I had two teenage sons. Not relishing the idea of being gone from them for the duration of my study, I dragged them to Mongolia for a couple of lengthy stays to work and live with me under very rough conditions. So it surprised me a little when ten years later one of them decided to undertake a snow leopard study of his own for his master's degree research. As science and conservation director for the Snow Leopard Trust, it was lucky for me that he made that decision exactly when I needed someone for the Kyrgyzstan study. Candidate number one: my younger son, Kyle McCarthy.

About a year earlier I had hired a young Kyrgyz biologist, Kubanych Jumabay, the same age as Kyle and also a graduate student, to assist the rangers and scientific staff of the Sarychat Ertash Reserve in setting up a program to assess the impacts of a gold mine on the edge of the reserve. During that first year he proved himself beyond expectations, conducting surveys of wild sheep and goats and tracking snow leopards for weeks in the remote mountains around the mine. All the while I don't think he ever stopped smiling, which somehow seemed to make up for the fact that he spoke little English. He did good work and was having fun doing it, and I was having as much fun training him. When Kyle said he needed a counterpart to work with, someone who spoke at least a little English, I knew who to ask. Candidate number two: Kubanych Jumabay.

By summer of 2005 the study was ready to launch. A half-ton of equipment and food was staged at the Sarychat Ertash headquarters. Kyle and his new wife, Jennifer, had arrived in Kyrgyzstan and, along with Kubanych, were about to head to the peaks for months of groundbreaking research. I was there to see that everything started smoothly and then leave them to it.

Arrangements had been made for a truck from a nearby gold mine to take us and the gear to the end of the road, high on a mountain pass. There we were to be met by rangers on horseback, who would take us the rest of the way to the planned base camp. We left for the pass early in the morning, stopping after three hours at the military outpost that monitors access to the border area in which the reserve sits. I stepped out along with park staff who handed our papers to the military guard. Although the conversation was in Kyrgyz, I could tell it wasn't good. We were lacking one government stamp and were denied access. That did not sit well with me, after all the effort that had gone into ensuring a smooth start. These were my staff; how could they have neglected to get the required stamp? I started to argue with the border guards, but then I heard Kyle say very calmly, "Dad, it's my study, let me deal with it." I started to protest, but I could see that doing so was not to Kyle's liking, so I walked back to the truck and tried to calmly read my book. An hour and several futile satellite phone calls to our office later, we were on our way back to park headquarters, losing a day to get the one stamp we lacked.

The next day things went better, and we were allowed into the reserve. When we reached the pass early in the afternoon, we found no rangers there to meet us. Since we needed to get the truck back to the mine before dark, a half-ton of gear and the research team were deposited on a muddy plateau just as a wet summer snow started. An hour passed, then two. I again began to quiz my staff rather forcefully about this latest planning failure, and once again I heard Kyle say very calmly, "Dad, it's my study, let me deal with it." I sat on my pack and tried to read my book in the snow. Eventually the rangers arrived, and, with a string of heavily laden pack animals, we descended the pass and arrived at camp several hours after dark. The acrid smoke of a dung fire mixed with the aroma of boiling mutton never smelled so good.

I stayed in camp for about a week, helping where I could, interfering more than once, but mostly watching two young biologists confidently going about their job. Kubanych kept smiling, and in his broken English he gave Kyle far more advice on how to set camera traps for snow leopards than I ever could have. He knew the terrain and the animal well, and Kyle knew the technology and the science behind his study—they made a formidable team. It was time for me to leave them to it.

Accompanied by a pair of rangers, I rode back toward the pass. Kyle, Jenni, and Kubanych accompanied me as far as the swollen river where we said our goodbyes. I reached the other side of the river and looked back. The three of them were trotting back toward camp, dwarfed by the thousand-foot peaks rising from the valley floor. A brief moment of apprehension hit, and I asked myself what I was thinking, leaving these young people—just cubs, really—out here on their own for months. Yet there it was all over again—youthful energy combined with defiant determination, sending a simple but clear message: "Left to ourselves we will be fine." My apprehension was quickly replaced by certainty in their skills and more than a little pride, and once again the long trek home was a whole lot easier.

Their study was a success and provided substantial insight into how best to monitor the conservation of snow leopards. Kyle continued to work on big cats as part of a postdoctoral study, and Kubanych became the leader of the Kyrgyzstan Country Program for the Snow Leopard Trust.

I stated at the outset that I consider myself exceedingly privileged to have spent a large part of my career studying and conserving snow leopards. I feel just as fortunate having worked with so many dedicated and capable people during that time, including most of the authors in this book. I was mentored by some of the best people in our field and am grateful for it. I hope in turn that I have shared something with the next generation, the cubs who will take the fight forward. There is much still to do.

KYLE McCARTHY

EPIPHANY

KYRGYZSTAN—*A young boy's destiny is revealed one cold winter night on a mountain in a distant land.*

Here I stand, in the middle of a small photo booth somewhere in the streets of Bishkek, the capital city of Kyrgyzstan; in my hands is the culmination of two months worth of backbreaking effort—a washed-out photograph of a snow leopard. I think to myself, a decade ago the snow leopard tore my family to shreds. So why am I here? Why have I dragged my new wife with me to the middle of nowhere? To a diet of rotten goat meat and moldy potatoes, a toilet of curved ibex horns over a shallow hole, tea strained through teeth in a vain effort to remove glacial silt, torturous days of hiking, worthless camp gear, and the nearest hospital two days away on horseback followed by an eight-hour jeep ride. What could possibly have led me to this remote, harsh world? The answer lies in the path my life has taken since childhood, leading me to an unlikely kinship with a rare cat. This cat, the snow leopard, guided me through sorrow to an awakening love.

When I was four, we loaded our family into a Volkswagen bus and moved to Alaska, living on Admiralty Island among the densest brown bear population in the world. My father gathered data for his master's degree while my older brother, Keegan, and I learned firsthand the ways of raw nature. But this is a book about snow leopards, so I'll fast-forward my story to the place of my freshman year in high school, the Gobi Desert of Mongolia. After years of flirting with charismatic animals from the wild lands of Alaska, I didn't expect to meet my first true love in the barren landscape of the Gobi Desert. I also never expected to cradle such an exquisite creature as the snow leopard in my arms, but I did.

I remember well the day my dad got "the call." In the world of wildlife biology, when you get a call like this it might as well be from the president. When the man on the other end of the phone is Dr. George Schaller, offering you a chance to work with him, you sit up and take notice. With few cat specialists in Mongolia, George needed someone to head a research study on snow leopards, and my dad was the man to do it. Suddenly, my family was leaving Alaska and heading to Mongolia. There we were, a few short months later, settling into a concrete flat in the middle of Bayantooroi, a small settlement in southwestern Mongolia, headquarters for the Great Gobi Biosphere Reserve and a stopover along the ancient Silk Road. One objective of the study was to learn whether the reserve had a healthy population of snow leopards and was large enough to protect them.

Our flat came with limited indoor plumbing, so the first major task in the study was to dig a hole about fifteen feet deep and four feet wide. We sunk an old coal chimney into the hole and lined the bottom with fresh hay. Next we built a wooden frame above the hole large enough to fit a full-grown man, then added a corrugated tin roof. Finally, we put a door on the entrance and carved a half moon into it. The first step in our fieldwork — the outhouse — was complete, and this was one of the best I had ever seen.

Unfortunately, we were not truly in the field yet but rather waiting in Bayantooroi for permits, waiting for staff, waiting to pick a study site, waiting to get over dysentery. Thank God for that outhouse. We waited so long that six months later I was on a plane back to Alaska with my disillusioned mother — life in Mongolia, not to mention field research, isn't suited for everyone and is certainly less glamorous than it might sound. We never set a single snare, let alone picked a likely study site. With my mother, brother, and me in Alaska and my dad half a world away in Mongolia, the high adventure of snow leopard research was replaced by the tears of a family divided.

Back in Alaska, my mother, brother, and I lived in a small apartment (we had sold our house to help fund our move to Mongolia). More tears. Back in Mongolia, my dad tried to cut through red tape while living on pennies, struggling to get to the only phone within 100 miles to call us as often as possible. In high school, somewhat bored, I was more concerned about fast cars and pretty girls than anything else. Two years later, little had changed. My dad managed to return from time to time for a month here, two months there. His absence left big holes in our lives. My dad had always been close to his kids. We missed building luge runs together in the winter, waking up at 6:00 a.m. to get to a ski race, hunting together, fishing together. In fairness, he thought we would all be with him through the duration of the study. None of us knew how hard that would truly be, but in retrospect I think not being together as a family was much harder.

I remember the next big call, even bigger than the one from George, only it wasn't by telephone; rather, it was a wakeup call: my parents were getting a divorce. They chose one of the few times my dad was back in Juneau to tell my brother and me. It was Christmas. Those damned snow leopards. More tears. A few months later I had to choose between returning to Mongolia with my dad to live in a ger (Mongolian felt tent), isolated from the world, wash in a hole cut through river ice, poop in a shallow trough cut into the rocky soil, and hike fourteen miles a day in the biting cold or move to New York City, live with my mom near the university, remain connected to the world, use a porcelain toilet, continue to pursue girls and fast cars. For an Alaska boy, the wilds of Mongolia easily trumped the big city.

We all have something in our lives that defines us, that directs us to follow a certain path. For me, it was this second trip to

Mongolia. During my sophomore and junior years of high school, computers interested me. I made little programs that could be mistaken for games. I also dabbled in robotics, winning a ribbon at the science fair for a search-and-rescue 'bot. For a while, I considered joining the Marines. But none of these paths struck me, moved me, consumed me. Sure, I had grown up around wildlife, with bears on the deck, owls and porcupines recuperating in the garage, all of which I had taken for granted. Though seasoned by the natural wonders of Alaska, I sensed that my true path, my passion, my destiny remained somewhere out there ahead of me. Mongolia beckoned. Though I didn't know it at the time, so did the snow leopard.

Back in Mongolia, we finally situated our research camp in the Saksai Valley somewhere in the Altai Mountains. It looks just like the valley next to it and the one after that and the next — barren, rocky, steep, coated with the hard bristle of a shrub that disdains leaves and the color green. Aside from a few nomadic camel herders, there were no people except us and no people in the next valley or the next — and did I mention that the Mongolian winter is cold?

We ran three trap lines out of our camp situated at the mouth of the valley, near our ready supply of frozen water from the river. I don't remember the exact number of snare sets but recall that they were spread out over a long distance. It was my job to get up in the morning and check the river-line sets, following the valley up toward its origin, a brisk five-mile jaunt. When I got back to camp we would eat breakfast, then head out together to check the longer, uphill ridgeline set, about twelve miles round-trip.

Hiking to check the sets honed our physical endurance, but it wasn't nearly as difficult as the waiting. Studying the snow leopard isn't like studying song birds, geckos, monkeys, or other small animals with small territories. You don't go out and run ten surveys and count dozens of little snow leopards. Instead, you hike for miles and miles, day in, day out, and see nothing. You do this for weeks, sometimes months. Snow leopards defy easy capture, easy study. They evolved over the millennia as stealthy, secretive creatures perfectly adapted to life in rugged mountains far from humans.

The waiting becomes so routine that when something finally happens it takes awhile for your brain to register it. We were on the long set, the one that ran up the ridgeline, four of us — my father, my brother, his friend Scott, and me. Someone stopped, shushed, holding up a hand. But by that point I was focused on the snare, or rather, where the snare should have been. This particular snare had been anchored to an old rusty axle, dropped off over some pothole years ago by a Russian jeep. It was plenty heavy; the indentured camel we used to drag it up the ridgeline could attest to that. The snare itself was tethered by aircraft-grade steel cable, meaning it was unbreakable. But as the old adage goes, a chain is only as strong as its weakest link; in this case the weakest link was a swivel, thoughtfully placed in-line with the steel cable to prevent twisting during a capture. Apparently, though, when jammed between two rocks and twisted sideways, it becomes no stronger than a safety pin — well, at least not as strong as aircraft-grade steel cable. We had finally caught something but that something was no longer there, only a lonely axle with the tag end of cable and half-swivel hanging from it — not a defining moment but rather an "oh shit" moment.

As Alaskans skilled in the finer arts of hunting and trapping and fans of John Rambo, we did what came naturally — we tracked our lost snow leopard. The snare and two yards of cable made tracking easier, but it was still an intense search. Whenever the trail petered out, things got really quiet until one of us would pick up a sign somewhere. Then we were off again. Darkness settled quickly on our mountain and our search, the kind of darkness one experiences only in the middle of nowhere. Headlamps came out and we continued. It got colder, as it can get only in the middle of a Mongolian winter. We carried on.

We knew the broken swivel wasn't the result of carelessness but rather was one of those numerous unforeseen conditions that happens in real-life fieldwork. Research study plans attempt to be comprehensive but, no matter how detailed, conditions on the ground can be unpredictable, even more so in remote and difficult terrain. We are visitors in the snow leopard's world. At times, we put ourselves at risk, but we do so willingly because these beautiful creatures need our help. We did not want to lose this cat. Mistakes happen, but we were determined to make this one right.

I nearly cried thirteen hours later when the leopard's trail finally ended. My tears were not from sadness but from jubilation—we had found our cat. A pile of boulders and giant rock slabs had toppled down the mountain, creating a field of uneven, leg-breaking peaks and crevices. A few came together, forming a winding tunnel, burrowing for fifty feet beneath rocks the size of houses. At places the tunnel was no wider than a man's hips, at other points you could nearly kneel, and at the end an angry snow leopard waited, wearing a shiny bracelet of steel.

My dad entered the tunnel headfirst, jab stick forward, drug loaded in the needle. My brother followed behind to hold the light and pass forward anything else that might be needed. I stayed above, following their progress by the sounds escaping from narrow slits in the joined rocks. When I heard the growling cat cornered in a cave, its only exit blocked by my father, I actually did cry. Luckily, snow leopards are not aggressive like other big cats, such as the mountain lion or tiger. They are actually rather docile and have never been known to attack humans. Scared and growly but docile. Soon she emerged cradled in the arms of my dad and brother, asleep to the world.

By this point we were all pretty keyed up and exhausted at the same time, our bodies and emotions near their limits. The poor snow leopard likely felt the same, but she had the release of a dissociative anesthetic mixed with a tranquilizer—she would remember none of this. Sitting there on the rocks beneath a blanket of stars over the Gobi, oblivious to the bitter cold and holding this magnificent creature, an awakening epiphany warmed me. At sixteen, I was the right age to fall in love, and I did. Not just with our cat, not even with snow leopards in general, but with nature, conservation, Mother Earth. Everything we had just been through, everything we had put the snow leopard through, all of it was aimed at saving these cats. We were working hard to keep this species around so generations to come might know they still roam free. I felt good.

I can't do full justice to that day and night in a few short paragraphs. It was raw, visceral, like the perfect novel. We struggled through so much, our plot line interwoven with that of the snow leopard, but in the end we were triumphant.

I came back from Mongolia with a new direction for my life. I dropped my ambitions to become a code monkey at a computer think tank, to build robots, to join the Marines. I was going to save the world, or at least whatever tiny piece of it I could. Earlier I mentioned that the snow leopard had torn apart my family. Whether that was true or not, I do know that it rebuilt, redirected my life. I moved to Fort Collins, Colorado, and enrolled at Colorado State University (CSU), where I met my wife, who is also a biologist. After CSU came graduate school and the chance to return to snow leopard country. Kyrgyzstan is both similar to and different from Mongolia, but wherever the snow leopard lives feels like home to me.

It was happening again: waiting, hiking, a shallow trough for a toilet, poor rations, and long days. Only this time, instead of snares we were using self-triggering remote cameras to "capture" snow leopards. Our images could be used to count individual animals and make hypotheses about their population. There would be no holding a snow leopard this time. But, when we finally got that first picture, the feelings from that night in the Gobi quickly returned: a bit of triumph, a lot of love. I held in my hands the first shot of a snow leopard taken in the Sarychat Ertash Reserve, and it was a beauty, even if a bit washed out.

At the start of my story, I questioned why I was in Kyrgyzstan. Similar questioning followed me to other places as well: vomiting on the border of Bukit Barisan Seletan National Park in Indonesia, exsanguinated by mosquitoes and black flies in New Hampshire bogs. Hardships merely test resolve, though. My resolve was forged one cold winter night in the middle of the Gobi Desert by a strange kinship with a rare cat—the snow leopard. That union lit a spark in me that has grown to a flame. Any world that harbors something as purely beautiful as a snow leopard is a world I want to be a part of, a world I want to take care of, a world I love.

SOM B. ALE

PANGJE

NEPAL—*In a mystical land of sacred valleys, a young biologist sets out to save the snow leopard and discovers in the process an ageless ethic that exists between the local Buddhist people and all living things, including the snow leopard.*

October 24, 2004. Dawn gradually approached as we gathered field gear to leave for our next camp in Phorche, a small Nepali village en route to the Everest base camp. A series of piercing whistles interrupted our work. Sensing something out of the ordinary, I hurried toward the sound and spotted five Himalayan tahr whistling alarms toward the nearby cliff. Crouched low, my field assistant, Lalu, and I scanned the cliff and surrounding slopes with binoculars. Nothing moved except the occasional startled flights of Impeyan pheasants. Far away, I could hear the faint echo of a herdsman yelling at his yaks. After half an hour Lalu whispered in my ear, "Something is moving on the rock." I slanted my spotting scope toward a cluster of boulders on the hedgy horizon. Something moved. I could hardly believe my eyes. A snow leopard came into focus, lying on a boulder, calmly grooming its paw. Several pheasants perched near the cat became abruptly noisy, their piercing calls penetrating the silence. The cat remained authoritatively unperturbed by the loud pheasants and jittery tahr. Suddenly, thin clouds moved swiftly across the entire mountain, briefly engulfing the drama before our eyes. The leopard rose abruptly, yawned, and then ambled toward us. Hands unsteady with excitement, I managed several pictures. In and out of a veil of wispy clouds, the ghostly apparition moved to the base of an overhanging rock, sniffed it, rubbed its left chin, then turned its rear toward the rock and sprayed—an invitation to mate or a cautious warning to competitors. After nearly twenty minutes it moved slowly out of view, leaving me breathless, heart pounding . . . quiet. After ten years I had finally witnessed the spirit animal of Nepal's great mountains.

My first sighting of a snow leopard happened near Mount Everest, but my first introduction to snow leopards in the wild came a decade earlier in the Annapurna region of north-central Nepal. Like any fresh, enthusiastic university graduate who dreams of a wildlife career, I eagerly accepted a post offered by the Annapurna Conservation Area Project (ACAP), established to protect the natural and cultural resources surrounding the Annapurna Himal, which includes the tenth-highest summit in the world. As Nepal's most popular trekking destination, the region is experiencing increased socioecological impacts from the trekking industry. Tourism in Nepal originated in the Annapurna area, popularized when Maurice Herzog, a French mountaineer, reached the summit of Annapurna I in 1950—the first-ever ascent of a 26,000-foot peak. News of Herzog's feat exposed a mountain paradise to the world. The number of trekkers swelled, bringing opportunities and changes to thousands of farmers and shepherds living in the shadow of Annapurna. This remote land of geological extremes thwarts large-scale development, but even small disturbances can cause lasting environmental damage. My job was to convince villagers that conservation measures could improve their lives over the long term, offering ways to manage swelling tourism while simultaneously protecting natural resources—including the endangered snow leopard.

In the early 1990s a Japanese filmmaking crew trekked to Manang, a small village of 500 flattop roofed houses situated at the base of the Annapurna massif, about a five- to six-day walk up the Marsyandi drainage. Near the village, the crew baited live goats to attract snow leopards for filming. In an ironic twist, the filmmakers who studied and made the snow leopard famous inadvertently increased its peril: residents of Manang believed the use of local livestock to attract snow leopards made them less afraid of humans and more likely to poach other livestock in broad daylight. Villagers complained to ACAP, which hired a new staff person — me — to deal with this problem.

I was thrilled but also anxious about my new responsibility. Local inhabitants of Manang were rumored to be unfriendly to visitors. My four years among them proved the rumor to be unfounded. Time passed wonderfully as some of the wisest men I have ever met filled me with ageless stories about this valley of awesome mysteries — Bön deities, Buddhist lore, sky burials, and the mystical snow leopard. Folklore warned herders not to roast meat in alpine pastures; otherwise the mountain god would send its "dog" — the snow leopard — and the family would suffer livestock losses. Snow leopards and domestic cats are believed to have been born to remove the sins of past lives; therefore, killing one of these animals means its accumulated sins will be transferred to your own life. Other lore describes the snow leopard as a living "fence" for crops, meaning that in the absence of snow leopards, livestock would range free and thereby likely invade crop-fields. Above all, I came to know and appreciate the role of religion in the daily lives of mountain people. The Buddhist concept of dependent origination envisages the human species as existing in a unity of interdependence with all other beings and encourages humans to protect the delicacy of nature. A local fable about Milarepa, an eleventh-century Buddhist poet-saint, illustrates the concept: "One day, hundreds of years ago, a tribal hunter, Keragomba Dorje, was hunting in an alpine meadow. The hunter, chasing a wild blue sheep, came upon Milarepa deep in meditation. Before the hunter could kill his prey, the thoughtful Lama persuaded him not to do so."

That day, a hunter became a conservationist. A sacred cave of Milarepa's disciple attests that the lessons of Milarepa continue in the Manang Valley, where nature is still considered the abode of the spirit world and all animals are divine. Yet amid lore rich in reverence for all living things, the snow leopard continued to menace. My task was to praise the snow leopard and extol its virtues as a regulator in the web of life supported by the high mountains. Perhaps I tried too hard, talked too much. The local people nick-named me "Pangje," which means snow leopard. I accepted the name with pride and as a reminder of my purpose among them.

Ecologists recognize that wild predators influence the struc-ture and dynamics of populations and communities, which in turn modulate ecosystem health. But how do you relate that value to a herder who just lost his yak to a snow leopard? Local people become exasperated with conservation evangelists who preach predator protection. On one occasion I faced a drunken "stakeholder" who brandished a knife and threatened to toss me into the river several hundred feet below. Biodiversity conservation smacks of luxury to local people barely meeting basic needs. Until someone demon-strates the direct link between biodiversity and human welfare at a timescale of less than a generation, perhaps we will not be very effective in drawing the attention of policymakers, politicians, and villagers alike. This is the challenge we should all accept, but frus-tratingly little has been achieved in that direction. An appropriate parable is that of the frog in a pot of water: drop a frog in boiling water, and it will jump out immediately; place it in the pot and slowly heat the water, and the frog will cook before it realizes its option to jump out. We know that we are slowly being cooked by what we are doing to the earth. Nobody minds a slow death; we all are slowly dying anyway. Conservationists can't seem to trans-late the boiling point of poor earth stewardship, especially without tangible links to the stock market. This should be our continuing quest: to find the best ways of waking and engaging people in a new relationship with the earth. My quest toward this goal would eventually lead me back to school and to yet another sacred mountain, Mount Everest—Mother Earth's highest point.

In Nepali, Mount Everest is called Sagarmatha, or Qomolangma by local Sherpa people. By the 1960s snow leopards were rumored to have disappeared from the region for reasons unknown today.

Himalayan tahr, a key prey of the snow leopard, was also at record lows. "Thirty years ago, you would never see *rerau* [local name for tahr] around the way you see them today, carefree of foreign trekkers or passersby," an old Sherpa told me. He added, "Army hunted them all." Ironically, with the establishment of Sagarmatha National Park in 1976, the Nepal Army was tasked to protect the animals it sometimes hunted. With strict laws and regulations enforced, conservation efforts took hold. The late 1980s witnessed a few scattered snow leopard sightings. My sighting described in the essay's opening paragraph made international news. The snow leopard's food sources, tahr and musk deer, were also making a comeback.

Although it was thrilling that the snow leopard had returned to Mount Everest, conservation challenges lay ahead. How do people cope with snow leopards that kill their livestock? The recovery of wildlife in Mount Everest was credited in part to Buddhist bans on hunting and slaughter. Would the Buddhist sentiment toward snow leopard predation hold over the long term? I found that most Sherpas, the predominant ethnic group in the Everest region, possessed a benevolent attitude toward snow leopards. When asked "Is the snow leopard a God?" some replied that it is "god of the mountains," while others considered it the "dog of the god." "Snow leopard is our deity . . . it protects our dharma from deviation to undesirable directions," monks and village elders exclaimed. This was music to my ears, for as in the Annapurna region, the Buddhist interpretation of nature can be a powerful influence, ascribing harmony over harm. Carried forward for generations, Buddhist traditions and teachings bring origin and lineage to the great mountains and magical valleys.

Long ago, the great saint Guru Rinpoche brought the teachings of Buddhism from India to Tibet and the Himalayan region. Out of the mountains he plowed 108 *beyuls,* or sacred heavenly valleys, empowering each of them with food and everything needed for meditation and spiritual progress. They were kept secret and were to remain hidden until a time of unprecedented religious crisis, protecting dharma until the misfortune passed. Rolwaling and

Khumbu, where Mount Everest stands, were said to be *beyuls*, the fabled Shangri-la or Shambala. These valleys are protected from the world by the mountain gods. Only the true followers of Guru Rinpoche, those who really practice his teachings, can find the sacred beyuls. If people with ill intentions try to find them, snow leopards will attack at the mountain passes and drive them away.

Rolwaling enjoys a sacred status among Sherpa. In this beyul, buried among dramatic landscapes, lofty peaks, and mysterious lakes, they seek transcendent reality and inner renewal. Rolwaling shares in the sacred charisma of the Himalayas, where giant glaciers feed the sacred Indus, Ganges, and Bhramaputra Rivers and fuel the South Asian monsoon—the foundation of agriculture throughout the region. It's no wonder the Himalayas are revered by hundreds of millions of Hindus and Buddhists as the home of gods. Rolwaling's tallest mountain, Tseringma, revered as Gauri Shankar by Hindu devotees, is believed to be the eldest of five divine sisters; one sister is reputed to reside on the summit of Mount Everest. Khumbila, Khumbu's country god, is identified as one of the twenty-one Bön demons Guru Rinpoche subdued and recruited to protect Buddhism.

Amid these soothing fables, my mind kept returning to the enduring ecological quest for balance between the snow leopard and people. With the return of the snow leopard, Sagarmatha faced new challenges. The park is too small to hold viable snow leopard numbers. Would this reestablished population serve as an impetus for re-colonizing adjacent areas outside the park? While my interest in and awareness of maintaining dharma were always on the rise, I wanted to visit this remote hermit land—not to seek ways to achieve nirvana but rather to explore whether the blessed valley remained a haven for the rare snow leopard.

I went to Rolwaling in October 2009 in search of the snow leopard. To my surprise, this narrow valley was moister than I had imagined and disappointingly devoid of the features snow leopards prefer. We looked for snow leopard markings, especially scrapes, along landforms such as ridgelines and along cliff bases. The entire place looked like a gigantic block of cliff. Snow leopard expert Rodney Jackson suggested that if snow leopards occurred in Rowaling, they would be found only in Na, a relatively open alpine valley. So our crew decided to move on to Na. The valley's east-west orientation would make it a convenient corridor for snow leopards.

After eight days of our arduous search for snow leopards in Na, we had yet to discover a clear snow leopard pugmark (footprint). We came across other signs such as feces and scrapes, but the elusive ghost did not leave behind its pugmarks. That day we climbed about 100 feet up the rugged, moraine hills, one after another, to reach the sacred glacial Omai Tsho, or Milk Lake, at 1,500 feet. Low and behold, we saw a clear set of footprints, likely an adult, along the airy beach. Local herdsmen reported snow leopard pugmarks on the pass leading to Mount Everest, but so far we had come across none. But our discovery at Milk Lake indicated that snow leopards may indeed travel to and from Mount Everest—an exciting find. Our Sherpa guide made a candid joke: "*Sarken* [snow leopards] go across the high pass; they don't suffer the altitude sickness as you lowlanders do." I agree with the local people: snow leopards move between Khumbu and Rolwaling. Earlier, there was a snow leopard kill on the Khumbu side of the pass. Along a ridgeline we encountered several scrapes and feces. Snow leopards were regular visitors here. This was surprising because this rolling terrain supports no tahr, and fifty years ago there were naur (blue sheep) here. Local shepherds occasionally collected the huge curved horns of blue sheep. Does Milk Lake and the surrounding area serve as a snow leopard refuge? Perhaps. Blue sheep are now locally extinct, likely because of the melting of glaciers that may once have facilitated wildlife movement from Tibet—the effect of climate change.

One day we located fresh snow leopard feces in broken terrain at the entrance to Na, near the monastery. Nearby on the mountain, above a famous boulder, is a cave where Padma-Sambhava practiced magic, *Phurba,* and left his footprint. During special festivals, all villagers go to the cave to perform ceremonies and make offerings. The entire sacred territory around the monastery and the magical sacred boulder is coincidentally the best snow leopard habitat in Rolwaling. So, for a week we set up camera traps, hoping the snow leopard would make its majestic appearance. It did not. Right across the river from this site is a huge rocky cliff the Sherpa say is the entrance to the inner valley. Villagers told us there are many wonderful and blessed caves with springs inside, where wandering yogis and ascetic practitioners spend long periods in meditation. I made a cursory visit to this area but encountered no snow leopard signs.

I noted Rolwaling as a strategic location for dispersing snow leopards from Mount Everest. Rolwaling herders reported the presence of at least three snow leopards, but we saw evidence of just one adult amid their several elusive signs. The second day of my descent from Rolwaling on the way to Kathmandu, along the noisy Bhote Koshi River with its tumble of rounded rocks, I lingered for awhile to watch ploughing going on in the nearby field. Every one of the workers and animals was covered with dark liquid mud, which was fine for the men in loincloths but may not have been pleasant for the women in their voluminous skirts. This picturesque portrait of harmony between nature and humans was wonderfully soothing. For a moment I wished I could take part in the work and blend into the harmonious picture. Yet I knew the picture was deceptive. Real harmony will not be achieved until better ways are found to link conservation to people's livelihoods and, on the global scale, to the world economy. It is a daunting task that must be faced with ingenuity and humility. My experience suggests that the Himalayan mountain people, with their Buddhist faith and traditions, can help ecologists like me find the right path forward.

NOVEMBER 13

NEPAL—*The author shares a day in his epic odyssey of spirit to the Land of Dolpo, an enclave of true Tibetan Buddhist culture and mountain home of the elusive snow leopard. On this day he revels in the up-close observation of blue sheep, the snow leopard's favorite prey. It is another day of not seeing a snow leopard, yet day's end brings a satisfying, unexplained contentment. (Reprinted from* The Snow Leopard *by Peter Matthiessen.)*

The last fortnight has been clear and warm, day after day, but early this morning there were wisps of cloud, which could mean a change in weather. On these last mornings, just an hour after sunrise, sun and moon are in perfect equilibrium above the snows to east and west. High cirrus in the north, seen yesterday, foretold a drop in temperature: it is 12 degrees Fahrenheit this morning. The wind on Sonido Mountain has a hard bite in it, and the lizards have withdrawn into the earth.

From sunrise to sundown I move with the Shey herd, which has been joined in recent days by the band of rams. The herd is up at snowline, to the eastward; this Somdo summit must be close to 17,000 feet. Climbing, I traverse the slopes with my zigzag technique, stopping and stooping and otherwise signaling to the browsing sheep that I am but a harmless dung-seeker, like other Homo sapiens of their acquaintance. By the time I arrive at snowline they have started to lie down; I reach a lookout knoll perhaps 150 yards away. The animals will feed again in the midmorning, then rest through the noon lull, then feed intermittently until sundown.

A little past ten the sheep begin to browse, at the same time paying close attention to the other animals. Though now and then two females chase each other, the activity is mostly among the males—male mounting male, and rampant rump rubbing, and some mild shoving. There is a "pairing" that becomes apparent when one spends the entire day with a single group: the males that test each other, shove, mount, butt, and rob, also seem to feed and rest together and, furthermore, are very alike in size of horn, development of black display markings, and dominance position in the herd; these trial confrontations and approaches are almost never between mismatched pairs.

Nibbling the snow patches and pawing up dust before settling gracefully, bent fore-knees first in the warm sun of a hollow, out of the wind, the animals have let me come so close that I can admire their orange eyes and the delicate techniques of horn-tip scratching, as well as the bizarre activities centered on the hindquarters of both sexes: at this early stage in the progress of the rut, the recipients of rump rub and urine check pay little heed or none to their admirers. Meanwhile, the yearlings scamper prettily to stay out of the reach of itching adults. There has been no real fighting or advanced sexual display of the sort that is beginning to be seen in the western herds, although occasionally a male will approach a female slowly, his extended neck held low, in what GS [George Schaller] calls "low-stretch" behavior, an overture to copulation. Since the Somdo herd has grown so used to me that I can observe it comfortably without binoculars, it is a pity that I must leave before full rut.

Toward noon there comes cold wind from the southeast, quite disagreeable on this bare scree slope, without cover, and, getting chilled, I ease the herd downhill and to the westward simply by crowding it a little, on the lookout for a rock or tussock shelter. The herd pauses for an hour or more on a flat ridge while I lie back snugly against my rucksack in a dense clump of honeysuckle just above: directly below lies the Crystal Monastery, with the home mountains all around, the sky, and as the sheep browse I chew dry bread in this wonderful immersion in pure sheep-ness.

In midafternoon, in a series of exciting flurries, I move the sheep farther downhill again to where GS, on his return from the Tsakang slopes, might study them without making a long climb. Then Old Sonam [elder woman resident near Crystal Monastery], out hunting dung, scares the herd back toward the east. The animals are flighty now, and so I stalk them with more care, rounding the mountain and crawling upwind to a tussock within sixty yards of the small rise where they stand at attention, staring the wrong way. Now and then, a head turns in my direction; I stay motionless, and they do not flare. The creatures are so very tense that even the heavy horns bristle with life. No muscle moves. For minute after minute I watch the roughing of their coats by the mountain wind.

Thinking to move them back toward the west I sit up slowly, and all turn to look. But the contrary beasts, having fled so often for no reason, confound me once again. With a man popping up almost on top of them, they now relax a little and begin to feed, as if the suspense of not knowing where I was had been what bothered them. They even start to lie down again. Cold and fed up with their lack of behavior, abandoning all hope of witnessing goatish outrages unknown to science, I shoo them rudely toward the village. This time they run a quarter mile, straight to a rock outcrop just east of the first houses.

I descend the mountain to the Saldang path, turn west toward Shey. Already the path lies in twilight shadow, but the rocks on which the blue sheep stand, not thirty yards above, are in full sun. And now these creatures give a wild sunset display, the early rut that I had waited for all day. Old males spring off their rocks to challenge other males and chase them off, and young males do as much for the females and young, and even the females butt at one another. Unlike the true sheep, which forges straight ahead, the bharal, in its confrontations, rears up and runs on the hind legs before crashing down into the impact, as true goats do—just the sort of evidence that GS has come so far to find. The whole herd of thirty-one joins in the melee, and in their quick springs from rock to rook, the goat in them is plain. Then one kicks loose a large stone from the crest, scattering the animals below, and in an instant the whole herd is still. Gold-eyed horned heads peer down out of the Himalayan blue as, in the silence, a last pebble bounces down the slope and comes to rest just at my feet.

The bharal await me with the calm regard of ages.

Have you seen us now? Have you perceived us?

The sun is retreating up the mountain, and still the creatures stand transfixed on their monument of rock.

Quickly I walk into the monastery to tell GS he can study his *Pseudois* by poking his head out of his tent. But a note says that in the hope of photographing the snow leopard he will sleep tonight across the river near the Tsakang trail: with a creature as wary as this leopard, there is no place for two.

If all else fails, GS will send Jang-bu [head Sherpa] to Saldang to buy an old goat as leopard bait. I long to see the snow leopard, yet to glimpse it by camera flash, at night, crouched on a bait, is not to see it. If the snow leopard should manifest itself, then I am ready to see the snow leopard. If not, then somehow (and I don't understand this instinct even now) I am not ready to perceive it, in the same way that I am not ready to resolve my *koan*; and in the not-seeing, I am content. I think I must be disappointed, having come so far, and yet I do not feel that way. I am disappointed, and also I am not disappointed. That the snow leopard *is*, that it is here, that its frosty eyes watch us from the mountain—that is enough.

At supper the Sherpas, in good spirits, include me as best they can in their conversation, but after awhile I bury myself in these notes so that they can talk comfortably among themselves. Usually this means listening to Tukten, who holds the others rapt for hours at a time with that deep soft voice of his, his guru's hands extended in a hypnotizing way over the flames. I love to watch our evil monk with his yellow Mongol eyes and feral ears, and it is rare that I look at him when he isn't watching me. One day I will ask this yellow-eyed Tukten if, in some other incarnation, he has not been a snow leopard or an old blue sheep on the slopes of Shey;

he would be at no loss for an answer. At supper, he regards me with that Bodhisattva smile that would shine impartially on rape or resurrection — this is the gaze that he shares with the wild animals.

DARLA HILLARD

WINTER AT CHÖRTEN NYIMA

SIKKIM, NEPAL, TIBET—*At a sacred pilgrimage site, winter grants a young Buddhist nun a reprieve from the changes in her world as growing blindness deepens a spirit-filled life.*

In today's world, Chörten Nyima (Sun Shrine) lies at the place where the borders of Sikkim, Nepal, and Tibet come together. But the known history of this major Tibetan power place goes back thirteen centuries, to the time when miraculous deities carried precious relics from India on a ray of sun and deposited them at the site of Chörten Nyima. Sacred phenomena abound here: a crystal that came on the ray, medicinal springs, and an oracle lake that can foretell the future to those with a particularly pure mind.

Conversely, a pilgrimage to Chörten Nyima, and a bath in the oracle lake's freezing waters, is said to wash away defilement and sin.

The remarkable explorer Alexandra David-Neel visited the monastery in the early 1900s and wrote about the four nuns she found in residence: "Numerous examples of strange contrasts are to be seen in Tibet, but what astonished me was the tranquil courage of the womenfolk. Very few Western women would dare to live in the desert, in groups of four or five or sometimes quite alone.

Few would dare . . . to undertake journeys that last for months or even years, through solitary mountain regions infested by wild beasts and brigands. This shows the singular character of Tibetan women." David-Neel could have been describing herself.

Rodney Jackson and I were drawn to Chörten Nyima in the summer of 1997. Mountain monasteries and sacred sites all across central Asia lie in prime snow leopard habitat. The human guardians of these sites have coexisted with and protected the nearby wildlife. We thought that a place so revered, so remote and harsh for human beings, would surely support good numbers of snow leopards and their wild prey. We knew that a road now led to Chörten Nyima. No one had mentioned that a mineral water-bottling factory now harnessed the sacred spring.

We, too, found nuns caring for the monastery that had been destroyed in China's Cultural Revolution and rebuilt in recent years. The head nun talked to us about the wildlife she no longer saw in the warm months—not because she was going blind but because of the noise and the influx of factory workers. Winter, she said, is the time for the blue sheep and the snow leopard.

We cannot know what beliefs were held by those who established Chörten Nyima more than a thousand years ago, but we do know that indigenous people have regarded powerful felines as both protectors and unifiers of humankind. On the day we walked high above the monastery, two things were on my mind: the wish to see a snow leopard, and the certainty that the oracle lake's gift of clairvoyance was not for me. I don't want to see the future. But something unexpected did happen. I could not get Chörten Nyima out of my mind, its aura of otherworldliness and antiquity. Something had shifted within me, like an eye beginning to open, a glimpse not of the future but of time immemorial.

> She wakes at first light, glides
> catlike to the fireplace
> to coax lumps of dung to flame.
> Above the monastery, snow pyramids slice
> the blue-gray Tibetan sky.
> Only their peaks catch the sun.

Shivering, she winds the sash of her red woolen robe
snug against her waist. A prayer-chant
tumbles softly from her lips.
She cups icy water to her face,
working instinctively, anticipating
her encroaching blindness.
She is only 28.
No pilgrims, packed into trucks
spewing diesel smoke and raising the dust,
will come today
seeking absolution for their sins.
No workers will come to the factory squatting
concrete and incongruous beside the red-mud monastery,
turning sacred water into corporate gain.
There will be no clatter and thump day and night
from the monstrous generator,
like a wrathful god entrapped
in this factory's strange twist on the concept of defilement.
Six peaceful months in winter's white embrace.
Perhaps the last.

She tucks a pouch of barley flour into her robe
and slips out the gate.
She follows the motor road
and an unfathomable sense of urgency.
She notes the summer tracks
of farmers and herders
who came by the hundreds seeking solace
from the sacred surroundings of Chörten Nyima.
Fresher animal tracks overlay the human ones —
wild blue sheep down from the alpine meadows
in search of snow-free pasture; they seem to sense
their safety in the cold, quiet months
of stilled Chinese rifles.
And she notes bigger tracks, seldom seen,
of the argali sheep
whose refuge lies within Sikkim,
beyond the high peaks.

Heading for the massive glacier at the valley's head,
she knows she would scarcely need her own eyes here

had the monastery not lost its heart
to the madness of the sixties
and the uncertainties of her own lifetime.
On one hand she names the nuns who remain
in the rebuilt temple;
the Rinpoche — enlightened master — long since gone,
the other monks gone more recently;
no one under eighteen permitted — under the latest government
    edict —
to stay.
In an hour she reaches the sacred spring, drinks,
feels the flow of a millennium since Guru Rinpoche,
bringing Buddhism to Tibet,
stuck his staff into the ground
and brought forth the clear water.
She strokes the tangle of sun-bleached *lung ta,* prayer flags,
strung through the centuries across the spring,
layer upon disintegrating layer, the newest
flying free — red, blue, green, gold, white — colors of earth and sky
snapping in the wind.
She steps around the litter of cast-off clothing,
wooden bowls, and other personal symbols of sins
shed by the pilgrims.

The trail heads steeply up the moraine,
through wind-blown snow
and a garden of miniature *chortens,*
stones stacked one-on-one.
Topping the first rise, she looks down
into a small frozen lake.
The trail ahead is icy, treacherous,
but she knows the way, ignores the cold.
She stands at last at the edge of Guru Latso,
the oracle lake
fed by the towering glacier whose snout lies submerged
on the opposite bank.
Here is the source of the sacred spring,
provider of future knowledge
to those who can read its surface
now blue-white and deeply frozen.

The lake sings, a high-pitched zing of cracking ice.
Through the tunnel of her diminishing sight
she scans the ice wall,
notes each blue-vein permutation,
memorizing, as countless times before,
the soft edges and white pillows
that belie the glacier's pure and powerful force.
She turns, catching a movement—
the infinitesimal cat-twitch of a tail.
A snow leopard sits quietly nearby,
charcoal dapples on smoke-white fur.
A shadow on the snow.
It holds her in its steady gaze.

She is not alarmed;
there is no threat in this encounter.
Only the slow absorption of her urgency
and an ancient promise
within those amber eyes.

THE SPIRIT OF BAGA BOGD

MONGOLIA—*In the middle of a difficult study, a renowned snow leopard biologist makes an unusual find in the desert.*

I had no way of knowing, when I received the gift of a jaguar head carved from greenstone, just how potent a force lived within that small talisman. He was given to me by my friend Apela Colorado, an Iriquois tribeswoman who uses her doctorate in social policy to promote consensus and collaboration between Western and indigenous scientists, by networking with shamans across the globe.

The day I met Apela, she sized me up for a few moments, then said she had something to give me. As she lit a dry sprig of cedar, she began—in the indigenous way of passing on a gift of power—to tell this story:

> Sheltered from the torpor of a Yucatan afternoon, I sat with Kin, a Mayan Jaguar shaman who had carved the amulet. Kin was barefoot and dressed in the traditional white tunic of a tribal elder. Wanting to bridge the language challenges, I opened my laptop to a photo of a snow leopard, tail held high, walking across a flat snowy patch. I told Kin about the traditional sacredness and the modern-day perils the cat faces. "This

amulet will go to someone protecting the snow leopard," I said, then asked Kin to pray for this person and for the cat. The old man leaned into the computer screen and looked as if to merge with the being on the screen. He stayed this way for several minutes, then leaned back slightly. Holding the amulet between his hands, Kin voiced a soft Mayan incantation. For a moment the surrounding jungle grew silent. Then he opened his hands, smiled, and placed the amulet in my hands.

Apela moved her hand through the cedar smoke and then placed the talisman in my hand. She closed my fingers around it and said, "Wear the jaguar close to your chest, out of sight of other people. This will help you, give you power, guidance, and protection when you need it."

Cat power. Shaman power. I wasn't sure if I believed it, but the little jaguar went with me to Mongolia just the same.

Baga Bogd is an isolated massif in Mongolia, linking the Altai and South Gobi Mountain ranges. Rising upward to rocky peaks of 11,000 feet, broken by deep gorges, Baga Bogd seems almost out of place on the flat surrounding desert. In Mongolian, *Baga* means young or small; *Bogd* means mountain, but it may also refer to a saint, a priest, or a sacred place. Baga Bogd is renowned for its geologically active fault and the deep fissures caused by a massive earthquake that struck the Gobi-Altai region on December 4, 1957, shaking people from their gers and sending massive boulders down from the mountaintops.

We—myself and my partner, Bariushaa Munkhtsog, a biologist with the Mongolian Academy of Sciences—knew that Baga Bogd was not prime snow leopard habitat, but it held the promise of revealing important information about how the cats eke out a living in these fragmented, isolated massifs in the South Gobi Desert. We theorized that Baga Bogd, separated by 30 miles or more from the nearest suitable habitat, offered a vital link to the core snow leopard populations along the Altai range westward to Russia. When Munkhtsog had visited Baga Bogd the previous spring, he found snow leopard signs in most places he checked. By radio-collaring the leopards that shared this massif, our study would complement another study 160 miles to the south, in a more accessible area that harbored a denser population of cats.

When we set up our camp at the entrance to one of many canyons penetrating the Baga Bogd massif, it was late August 2008, and the change of seasons was in the air. In addition to Munkhtsog, our team included his colleagues Naranbaatar and Gana, as well as a puma and jaguar trapping expert and a veterinarian from the United States. The first sign that things were not to go as planned was the paucity of fresh snow leopard sign, even high on Baga Bogd where patches of snow had lingered through the hot Mongolian summer and where one would expect a cat to hang out.

The roads, faint tracks across the desert, were strewn with boulders and dissected by deep flashflood-eroded gullies. Packed like sardines and sweating in the overheated Russian 4×4 van, we were tossed painfully in unison as we drove from base camp to places where we could begin to search on foot for suitable trapping sites.

Most of the canyons that penetrated Baga Bogd offered good prospects, but exploring them meant driving from the vast out-wash fan on which we were camped, down to the desert floor, then paralleling the mountain for three or six miles before heading back up to the next outwash fan and the canyon mouth. The driver had developed large biceps from wrestling the van's powerless steering system. He picked his way through knee-high sage and Caragana bushes, tumbleweeds, boulders, wild rye, feather grass, and loco-weed. The scent of sage drifted through the van's small side wings, the only windows that opened in a vehicle designed for cold Siberian winters. Stands of ancient poplar trees lined the entrance to each canyon, their gray trunks gnarled and fissured, their crowns ablaze with the first flames of fall color. Higher up, exposed ridges and cliffs of rust-colored rocks were broken here and there by steep gulleys with hanging boulders, effectively blocking our efforts to more thoroughly search Baga Bogd's high slopes and hidden alpine-like valleys. In the shelter of rocky amphitheaters, stunted groves of birch and willow showed fall colors noticeably advanced over the poplars.

At a herder's encampment, composed of several gers with circles of ground heavily trampled by large flocks of sheep and goats, we stopped to ask if any snow leopards or ibex had been spotted recently. Several women carried aluminum milking buckets, making their way along a double line of goats whose horns were tightly interlocked and ankles expertly tied during this daily pastoral routine. A cacophony of baahs and bleats announced the animals' empty stomachs and their wish to have the milking done so they could begin their daily trek to the mountain's green pastures and the freshwater springs that flow down the canyons, disappearing quickly beneath the desert sands.

Over the next three weeks we set out specially designed leg-snare traps, similar to those used by bear and cat researchers in North and South America. Yet we hardly ever found a site with the right natural features to funnel a passing cat so it would step precisely on the small, saucer-sized triggering device.

Early each morning we made the bone-jarring ride to monitor the traps, always hoping for a snagged cat. Then we spent the rest of the day looking for more sign, wishing for a fresh kill of ibex, the snow leopard's key prey. Placing a live trap beside a fresh kill is the ideal situation for catching a snow leopard; chances are the cat will return for another bite of its hard-earned meal. But we never found a fresh kill, only old bones remaining from ibex eaten earlier in the year.

Each evening we returned bruised, frustrated, and empty-handed. The weather was perfect, except for a few days of snow and the occasional windstorm that sent us rushing to anchor the three gers to the ground with rope and heavy rocks. The van balked at the way we were treating it and often broke down or simply refused to start. Its abused tires regularly went flat. It seemed the driver spent more time fiddling with the carburetor or blowing into a fuel line than actually driving. The van was a gas hog, and the nearest pump was a three-hour drive away, so Munkhtsog arranged to borrow a herder's motorized trail bike. After that, Naranbaatar could check the three traps we had placed along a well-worn trail in Ust (Water) Canyon, and we could avoid the daily forty-five-minute van ride. Like a wild Mongolian cowboy, precariously balanced and full of youthful abandon, Naranbaatar and the herder raced the little red Honda across the rocky alluvial fan, reaching the canyon's entrance in a mere fifteen minutes.

Day after day our traps were unvisited, the scant fresh sign leading us to wonder if the snow leopards may not have already been poached out. Were we simply too late? Nothing seemed to be working, not setting more traps, not "freshening up" scrapes with bobcat scent, not broadcasting recorded mating calls from snow leopards in the San Francisco Zoo to their Mongolian cousins.

As the odds of failure stacked up, divisions emerged within our small team. Cultural differences and egos played a part, along with the spartan camp conditions, the lack of snow leopards, and the mutton-and-vodka–heavy Mongolian diet. The condition of the local dogs was also an issue. The herders keep mastiffs to guard their gers, and many were missing a paw, having been caught in leg-hold traps set to kill wolves — creatures as deeply despised in Mongolia as they are elsewhere in the world. It seemed such a cruel fate, and how many snow leopards had been caught in those traps? As the team leader and the person most experienced with snow leopards, I sensed all eyes were on me to unify our team, to bring success.

Then one morning Naranbaatar returned from checking the traps and climbed off the motorbike with a deep frown on his sun-beaten brow. In a barely audible voice, he said that a snow leopard had been caught, but it had escaped and the opened snare cable was lying on the ground at the trap site. We were stunned. In disbelief, our trapper could not recall such an equipment failure, even with more powerful jaguars, and expressed his view that the cat had been taken by a poacher.

We sat in complete silence as the van ground its slow way to the trapping site. Arriving at last, we saw the opened snare cable with one of its retaining bolts loose, the cable's end frayed, no blood, and hardly any sign of a struggle, just as Naranbaatar had told us. It made no sense that this cat had escaped but it had, as if to show or teach us something.

I recalled from my trapping and radio-collaring experience in Nepal in the 1980s that snow leopards would often return to a trap site within a few days of their capture. So we set a new snare thirty yards away. This time we made sure the mechanisms were securely fastened, but we had little hope of a snow leopard paying a visit during the two days we had left. With other commitments and fixed airline flights, it would be impossible to extend our stay.

We went back to camp, dejected and frustrated. I had never felt so low during my thirty years of fieldwork. That afternoon I grabbed the shovel and plodded across the dry, dusty alluvial fan, heading for our pit toilet. My mind a jumble, I was cheered somewhat by the fragrance of prostrate rosemary plants growing in profusion among the low, lichen-encrusted rocks. Something in the trail ahead caught my eye, stopping me dead in my tracks.

There was a rock completely different from the other meta-morphic, well-polished, desert-varnished rocks scattered across the sands of the low ridge. It was about a yard long and as wide as a shoebox, partially embedded in the ground. It was a pale golden-coppery color with a flat surface pointing skyward. Across the surface ran the embossed shape of a serpent; it was banded in rich rust-brown and narrowly edged in the same color. I am not a geologist, but I instinctively knew this rock had to be one of a kind, not something thrown out by an ancient volcano. It bore absolutely no sign of aging from the intense desert sun or frigid winter temperatures. It was as if someone or something had planted it there. I walked this trail almost daily — how could I possibly have missed such an obvious and incongruous stone?

Awestruck, I knelt and gently moved my hand across the serpent's body to feel the texture and convince myself it really existed. I marveled at the snake's raised form, aware of its similarity to ancient images on sandstone walls in the American Southwest. At the same time I felt uneasy, tinged with renewed anguish at the discord within our group and deeply troubled by our failure to catch a snow leopard. I was keenly aware that we would soon have to pack our gear and leave Baga Bogd for good. How would I deal with our lack of success in collaring a cat?

I went on to the toilet pit, then returned to camp for my camera. I was back within the half-hour. The rock was gone. No, I thought, it must be here. It was so incredibly unlike all the other rocks, it should have been easy to find. I zigzagged back and forth. Nothing. The way to the toilet led straight from our camp across the slope, but I broadened my search to either side of the track. Nothing. I couldn't believe it. I wanted to keep searching but didn't want to let on to my teammates what had happened.

I went back for a remote camera trap and, not wanting to bring attention to my search, said I was scouting a spot to get a perfect picture of a pika posed beside the entrance to its burrow. These charming semi-colonial animals — more closely allied to rabbits or hares than to rodents — darted about the landscape, fleeing down one of their many holes whenever a person passed by or a raptor glided overhead.

I searched an area the size of a football field, systematically, as if running a scientific transect. But the more I searched, the more I knew I would never find that rock again. It had vanished as mysteriously as it had shown itself, just like the wild snow leopards I've had the privilege of glimpsing over my career. Finally, I gave up, sat down, and reached for the stone jaguar around my neck. I closed my eyes and cradled the talisman in my palm. A calming wave swept over me, flooding out the anxieties and difficulties of the past weeks. My mind shifted to simply being in the moment, and my sense of worldly urgency evaporated. I felt the timelessness of Mongolia, the land and the people. I thought of young Naranbaatar, whose ancestors would have lived following the guidance of shamans not so different from Kin, who had carved my jaguar.

Suddenly my peace of mind turned to joy, excitement, and the certainty that something momentous was about to happen. That night I slept the soundest I had on any night during the entire trip, despite the fact that we were running out of time and I would normally have been awake fretting.

We had just checked nearby traps the next morning when we heard Naranbaatar shouting over the noise of the dirt bike as he sped into camp. "Come quickly," he called, "we have caught a snow leopard!" We grabbed our equipment and piled into the van; for once, it took pity on us and started right up. We hardly noticed the bumps, engaged as we were in animated conversation, going over the immobilization procedures and what each of us had to do to ensure that the snow leopard had a smooth capture and a safe release.

We made the half-mile walk from the van to the trap site in what seemed like seconds, and there in the snare was a magnificent snow leopard. Quickly and smoothly, the veterinarian used a blowpipe to inject the tranquilizing drug. Within a few minutes the beautiful cat—an adult male weighing close to 100 pounds—was down, and we set about fitting his satellite radio-collar, taking vital statistics, applying medications, and taking photographs. Each of us had the pleasure of touching him and marveling at his deep, luxuriant fur.

When we were finished we invited the local herders, who had been quietly watching the proceedings from a distance, to come closer. It was surely the first time any of them had felt the quiet breathing of a live snow leopard through its soft fur. I wanted to do everything possible to ensure that this precious cat would be protected from poaching, especially from those awful leg-hold traps that had maimed so many dogs. We talked about the herders' responsibility to the leopard—their leopard—and how we had come into their community to share our knowledge and learn from them everything we could about snow leopards so the herders and the cats might better coexist.

Munkhtsog and his associates named the snow leopard Togoldor, which means very great, amazing, incredible. As we left him to recover in peace, we hung a white *kata* (ceremonial scarf) on a nearby poplar tree to honor the snow leopards as well as the mountain gods of Baga Bogd. Silently, I prayed that we could help the herders reclaim their belief in the right of Togoldor and the other wildlife to roam freely on Baga Bogd.

A year later, during which we tracked Togoldor's movements via the Internet, the electronic drop-off device functioned as scheduled, and the collar fell off his neck. Now we had the task of finding it somewhere in Baga Bogd's rugged terrain. Unbeknownst to us at the time, Togoldor had bitten off the antenna for the small VHF (very high frequency) backup transmitter intended to help locate the collar, and it was almost completely dysfunctional.

But luck or karma was on our side. Surprisingly, the satellite was still picking up the collar's transmissions every seven hours, even after the drop-off time had come and gone. From California, I could log on to the Internet site and receive a GPS coordinate. I e-mailed the precise location to Munkhtsog, who was in the field searching. At last, he and his associates recovered the collar from a narrow ledge high on a large promontory rock overlooking the desert plains above our abandoned camp. Had the collar fallen into a deep gully or with its satellite antenna facing downward rather than skyward, we never would have known where to look, as the satellite would not have received its signal. Yet it did work, maintaining a twenty-first-century link between me and a radio-collar halfway around the world. A strange-looking object on the outside, but inside it pulsed with energy, purpose, design. How incongruous it must have looked, should it have been seen by a passing person or beast. And, like the snake rock, it would have been there one day then gone the next, retrieved by Munkhtsog. I wonder what might have been radiating from the snake rock that I was incapable of sensing. Where and how did it vanish?

The collar contained an onboard chip that stored more than 1,100 locations, including the 170 or so downloaded to the Internet. These data have given us valuable insight into Togoldor's life. For the entire year, he never left the steep slopes of Baga Bogd in search of ibex, marmots, or a mate—except for once in the summer, many months after we had left, when he walked almost seven miles past our campsite to the open plains. But he quickly returned to the safety of his mountain refuge.

Since ancient times, big cats have had their place in the art and lore of human beings. The earliest evidence is found in southeastern Turkey at a site constructed more than 11,000 years ago. There, stone pillars were carved with animals that represented power and intelligence, including lions, foxes, and leopards. The snake, I have since learned, is universally a symbol of birth, new life, transformation, cosmic creation, and divine knowledge and wisdom. Our friend Apela, I have also learned, comes from a people who believe that rocks are ancient beings, that things move inside them, that they hear and record. Apela wasn't surprised about my shape-shifting rock or all that transpired during that field session in Mongolia.

And myself? I am still absorbing the shift that occurred within me, the possibility of my own connection to this other way of being in the world. I think of my greenstone jaguar talisman, resting in its box—a gift from my family in South Africa, decoupaged with a picture of a snow leopard hunting blue sheep in the Himalaya. I know that my new awareness comes with a deeper connection to snow leopards, to seek out more noninvasive methods of discovering their status in the wild, and my responsibility comes with a deeper obligation to form meaningful partnerships with indigenous people.

Cat power. Shaman power. I believe in it now.

D O N   H U N T E R

GOBI MAGIC

MONGOLIA—*As foretold, a journey to the desert delivers lively mental and physical stimulation . . . and a touch of magic.*

Each journey to the unknown begins by leaving the known. The familiar. The comfortable. Such thoughts filled my mind as I worked through my checklist for a field project in Mongolia. The last two items brought back the uneasy feeling in my stomach: #62 – photos of my wife and three small sons, from whom I would be away for several weeks. I culled pictures from family albums to a handful that made me smile and turned to #63: phone my family in Tennessee to check on my father. On my last visit a few months back, Alzheimer's disease had stolen his memory of me. His condition had not changed; I was wished safe travels.

At leaving time, our little "ranch" swirled with mixed emotions. My sons, ages six, three, and one, sensed the change in the normal rhythm of a peaceful world. "Daddy, where is Mongolia?" Daddy, how long will you be gone?" "Daddy, we will miss you." My wife Annie's assurance that she and the boys would be fine didn't assuage the heaviness on my heart. I was averaging one or two fieldtrips a year, having just returned from Pakistan a few months back. It seems everything in life comes with a price, even the good things. When I first began working internationally there were no kids; ten years later, my family owned my heart but competed with a rare cat for my time. When the kids came along, Annie and I agreed to a three-week limit on my trips, the minimum time to accomplish fieldwork but not the months some colleagues spend away from family. I wasn't resentful, but, in fact, each trip became harder as I missed seeing my sons grow.

As on each trip before, my guilt receded, goaded by an irrepressible, atavistic excitement about striking out on a journey to a new place, remote and faraway. I was aware that my battling emotions were not unique to me. At these times, I wondered where such intense feelings came from. My mind drifted to Homer's *Odyssey* and item #32 on my packing list: a good book.

I left my known, my familiar, in February, breeding season for the snow leopard, optimum time for capture work. Tom McCarthy had invited me to join him at his research camp in Mongolia's Gobi Desert. His radio-collared cats had ranged far from where they were collared, making it difficult to follow their movements. Tom and I believed satellite collars would solve the problem, so we each acquired one for his study. It was a grand opportunity for me: hands-on snow leopard studies are as rare as the animal itself.

I'm not superstitious, but I noted that my time in Mongolia coincided with Chinese New Year, 1996, the Year of the Rat, promising a time of "lively mental and physical stimulation." The first hint at such stimulation came in Beijing twenty-four hours later when I learned that my flight to Ulaanbaatar, Mongolia's capital city, had been cancelled: "So sorry Mr. Hunter, big problem, no flights, big problem, so sorry, it New Year, no flights." The Rat: after considerable physical and mental stimulation, I managed to catch the lone flight to Ulaanbaatar.

My host in Mongolia and Tom's resident science collaborator was Dr. Jachingyn Tserendeleg, head of the Mongolian Association for the Conservation of Nature and Environment, a very active nongovernmental organization. As the first Mongolian to work in the Antarctic and the country's chief endangered species expert,

Tserendeleg had earned great renown in Mongolia. I had met him a few years earlier at a snow leopard symposium in Xining, China. This highly accomplished conservationist drew me in, his fame and ego buried beneath genuine calm and confidence. His almond eyes the portals of a sanguine inner being, he was always quick with a contagious, full-faced Mongolian smile. I looked forward to getting to know him better.

After a breakfast of sliced meat, cheese, pickles, fruit, toast, and instant coffee presweetened and milked, I walked to Tserendeleg's apartment building a few hundred yards from my hotel, the cold February air assaulting my jetlag. Typical of Ulaanbaatar, the multistoried structure stood as a concrete reminder of Russian influence over politics and architecture, its cold exterior a stark contrast to the warmth of his welcoming family. I quickly became the American novelty and target of English practice. Badamsuten, his wife; two sons, Dasksa and Puujee; and daughter, Baroo, quickly made me feel welcome, the kind of welcome that strikes you immediately as sincere and familiar. The elder son Dasksa, with the best English, became the primary interpreter, as Tserendeleg and his wife spoke little English. "Welcome to Mongolia, so happy to meet you." "How was your journey?" "Do you have family?" "What are names of your sons and wife?" My short time with Tserendeleg's family, immersed in the love and laughter of daily life, comforted me against the deep winter cold and the loneliness of missing my family.

Mongolia's Tsagaan Sar (White Moon or White Month), though closely tied to the Tibetan New Year, falls concurrent with the Chinese New Year. Throughout the country the normalcy of daily life becomes punctuated with the rituals of the season. Since Tserendeleg is a national celebrity, knocks at his door continued through the evening, with well-dressed family and friends paying respects, repeating the time-honored traditions of the season: home and hearth clean and decorated, the family dressed in their finest, and a table laden with neat stacks of seasonal culinary delights that included colorful candy, savory breads, and all manner of drinks, topped with a lamb roast replete with the large tongue of rump fat balanced on top of it all. "*Sain baniuu*" (translated "How are you") starts the traditional exchanges of the season: the youngest drapes a silk scarf (*khadag*) over the extended arms of the elder, bows slightly, then kisses each cheek. The host and hostess distribute generous portions of sliced sheep fat, rich and healthful camel's milk, and *airag*, the common alcoholic spirit made from fermented mare's milk. Copious pourings of vodka lubricate convivial chatter. Even to sleepy foreign eyes, a very respectful, friendly, and fun celebration tradition.

To my surprise, my very early plane to Altay, the next leg of my journey, was only half full. I learned later that Mongolians are a superstitious lot and they eschew flying during the Tsagaan Sar. Our tired Russian twin-prop airplane offered a low, slow look at the Mongolian steppe. It looked like Wyoming on steroids, with fewer people. Widely scattered roads striped the countryside, with braided two-tracks running generally in a direction but not necessarily constituting an established highway. Our loud landing on Altay's gravelly airstrip woke me from a jetlag nap. My two large duffel bags were unloaded right at the plane; one in each hand, I worked my way to the small terminal room, anxiously looking for Munkhtsog, Tom's Mongolian field partner and my pickup man for the final eight-hour jeep ride to Saksi Camp, due south in the Gobi Desert.

Munkhtsog was a no-show. The Rat again. Outside in the parking lot I sat on my duffel bags, tired, despondent, perplexed, alone. I forced meditation. Constantine Cavafy's poem, "Ithaca," played in my head. Was this the adventure part, the instruction part, or just the long part? Eye contact with a couple staring at me from across the small parking lot broke my mantra of pity. Traditionally dressed in fine winter *deels*, calf-length tunics with colorful sashes, his deep burgundy, hers azure blue with a light blue print. Russian-looking Ushanka fur hats topped them both. They motioned for me to go with them. In the typical tourist loud-wills-understanding voice I said, "Hello, I am Hunter, you know Munkhtsog?" No reaction, so next I tried the slow-wills-understanding, "M u n k h t s o g?" They spoke no English but seemed to have identified me as their charge.

After awkward but cheerful greetings, we loaded their car for a short drive to their apartment on the third floor of another Russian multistory concrete icebox.

I was embarrassed that my luggage took up so much space in their small three-room apartment. They seated me on a sofa near one of the few, hazy windows. Soon there was a knock at the door: New Year's guests, of course. This time the ceremony included an offering of snuff by the host, contained in elaborately decorated tins stored in the *deel*'s generous sash pocket. Their table included steamed meatballs and greater quantities of mare's milk, the highest treat of all. It was a little after noon. Over the next five hours this warm, lavish, and convivial exchange took place another six times, always with the same sincerity and generous vodka toasts.

My tardy pickup man showed up at 5:30 p.m., just about the time warm meatballs, numerous vodkas, and monster jetlag had stupefied my brain. I gathered from Munkhtsog's choppy English that my host was an old classmate who had done him a favor by picking me up. After weeks in the field camp, Munkhtsog had taken advantage of being in town, making the rounds of his friends in Altay. He and our driver, also an old friend, were feeling pretty good by the time we finished yet another round of New Year's exchanges. Suddenly, Munkhtsog announced, "We go." With little fanfare, an aged Russian jeep was loaded and headed south into the night.

We had eight hours of travel ahead of us, beginning with a traverse of two mountain ranges between Altay and Tom's camp in the South Gobi. The tiny beams of light from our little jeep barely lit up twenty feet in front of us. I learned quickly that roads in Mongolia are more illusion than real, faint watermarks across a landscape so vast it engulfs you like a black hole. As we climbed and meandered through the mountains, our driver backtracked a couple of times and stopped several times, stepped out of the jeep, and stared at the night sky. At first I suspected a urinary problem or too much New Year's libation, but Munkhtsog told me this was the Mongolian way of travel—a combination of pilotage, celestial navigation, and old-brain knowing. "Mongolians never get lost," he assured me. Here, navigation had changed little in the past few thousand years. Whether by jeep, camel, or on foot, the way ahead rested in the hands of someone with an innate sense of direction, who can remember landmarks, judge distances, and read the stars. I mused that my passage so far had relied on radar, transponders, electronic receivers, instrument landing systems, and precise aerial maps, but the final leg of my journey called upon the stars. I couldn't decide whether to feel impressed or worried. On some higher slopes, snow had drifted across our path. We could plow through most of the drifts, but occasionally we had to get out and dig free. Our spartan jeep had no amenities like a heater or a radio. I rode in back, sitting on top of my duffle bags and other supplies for camp, fully wrapped in my winter gear—but still freezing. Munkhtsog and the driver seemed unaffected by the cold, laughing and talking as we jostled our way south.

On one of the navigation stops we got out to relieve ourselves, standing in a row facing south. The cold night air shocked my jet-lag into full remission. Eager to return to the car, our eyes were drawn to the sky—a swirling ball of light emerged from the south, so bright it clearly illuminated the vast floor of the Gobi fifty miles away. Like a giant heavenly sparkler, the spinning orb traversed the night sky right in front of us, slowly and without a sound, arcing northward, spewing trillions of brilliant white pieces of light until it finally dissolved into the dark northern horizon. In a celestial display of yin and yang, one minute our entire world was as bright as day, the next it was complete darkness. Heads cocked upward, mouths agape, we were speechless. My mind raced, searching for some rational explanation: meteor, falling star, piece of space junk, portend to apocalypse. I noted the time, 8:45 p.m., as we climbed back into the jeep. Munkhtsog and the driver had an animated discussion in Mongolian. Finally, Munkhtsog told me simply, "Strange things happen in Gobi; local people believe it is a magical place." What, I thought, could be stranger than that ball of light? They seemed content to let it go at that, with no more questioning, but I continued to replay in my mind the magnificent experience and my providence in witnessing such an awesome display of energy. True to the Rat, this night held way too much physical and mental stimulation. Soon we were winding our way down a mountainside, allowing my adrenaline-charged mind to focus on the knowledge that we were traveling through snow leopard country. Somewhere out there, one or maybe more of these illusive cats witnessed the light, just as we did. Were they as awed as we were, or were they in some way connected to the magic?

We stopped at a lone ger, the iconic symbol of the Mongolian steppe, alongside a frozen river. Camel parked outside, motorcycle parked inside. Changed little since the days of Genghis Khan, the round white ger appeared a natural part of the landscape. An elderly man greeted us warmly, along with his lovely daughter and three-year-old granddaughter. The leisurely rituals of Tsagaan Sar once again hoisted our spirits for moving on. The young woman and her daughter joined us. She might have been Munkhtsog's girlfriend, though I'm not certain. The bright February morning cheered us onward, happy travelers on a mission. Soon we broke from the foothills; the Gobi filled our view to the southern horizon. We stopped to stretch and gaze at the awesome vista. From where we stood, the Gobi continues beyond the horizon south for 500 miles, where it abuts the Kun Lun Mountains of western China. A couple of hours later we arrived at Tom's camp.

With great excitement, Tom and his sons described in minute detail the capture of *Char*, Mongolian for yellow, the general color of the snow leopard caught a week earlier. I was bummed to have missed out on the first capture but took heart that the next might happen while I was there. After lunch, I hiked the nearest peak for a look around and to clear my head, reeling from what seemed like nonstop travel, nonstop physical and mental stimulation for the past five days—Fort Collins, Tokyo, Beijing, Ulaanbaatar, Altay, the jeep, starlight navigation, the mysterious light. From atop the peak, facing into a cool wind, calm and warmth filled me. Down below I saw the small figure of a boy chopping away at the two feet of river ice, reopening the hole—a daily chore that supplied us with freshwater—the ger a small round dot beside the white Saksi River, snaking its way northward into the mountains. Out in the

Gobi, dominant in the southern vista rested "Mother Mountain," an exquisite monolith shaped like a giant female lying face upward on the desert floor, a sacred place, especially for Mongolian Buddhists. It felt good to meditate at this place. I wondered about the travelers who passed before me, journeying along this ancient trade route. I reflected on this opportunity to help a colleague, to put my education and experience to good use, to aid a species in need. The moment held me still, transcendent, like other instances where the quiet places of the snow leopard's world filled me with a sense of awe and gratitude, deeply satisfying a spirit sustained by equal parts mental and physical. At that moment it struck me: the Rat's message wasn't one of foreboding but rather a promise of spiritual fulfillment. I glanced downward and there, beside my booted foot, was a fresh snow leopard scrape.

Tom's camp reflected his Alaska field training: the well-organized ger brimmed with the accoutrements of daily life and wildlife research. The boys filled the camp with teenage energy. For Tom, too, the fieldwork had been difficult for his family, and there were problems. Yet despite the remoteness, his sons seemed to love roughing it in the middle of nowhere.

February in Mongolia brought mostly clear days and frigid nights, with temperatures in the early morning reaching about 1 degree Fahrenheit, warming through the day to a high of about 28 degrees Fahrenheit. Gers are marvelously adapted for holding up to the howling wind and bitter cold of the Asian steppe. It's easy to understand why they have changed little in thousands of years. Gers (called *yurts* in Turkic languages) function as versatile mobile homes for the nomadic. On a trip into the Kun Lun Mountains later in the year, we were forced to move our camp quickly ahead of a snowstorm. In less than an hour our fully furnished ger was neatly packed onto the backs of two Bactrian camels, Mongolia's four-legged pickup truck.

Day after day, the drill consisted of listening for Char's radio-collar and checking eighteen snare sets every day in hopes of catching a second cat. We rotated the duty of being the first up to start the cook fire and check the nearest traps. In the early morning, only noses stuck out of heavy down sleeping bags, but a small fire warmed the ger quickly. After breakfast, we set off to check the other sets, an uphill hike of several miles, listening for Char's signal as we hiked. It wasn't unusual to see an ermine scamper across the trail in front of us or old ibex horns scattered about, indicating a healthy population. The morning chill gave way to the sweat of upping the mountain. After a few miles, we shoved heavy coats into our backpacks, cooling to the second layer. On these hikes the smell of my own sweat reminded me to savor the physical part of my cerebral profession. I felt exuberant, lucky to have a job that challenged both worlds.

Char had not moved much since her capture. She was fairly old and Tom was concerned; he wanted to be sure she was okay. We set out one day to try to find her. At around noon we topped out on a ridge above Green Valley, where most of the remaining snare sets were located. Immediately, we picked up Char's beep, beep, beep from somewhere on the rugged hill slopes below. We scrambled down the slope, several times thinking we had her located, only to hear the beeps signaling out ahead of us. Tom and I moved downward around a small cliff face. The signal got louder, but we couldn't see her. Suddenly, like lightning, Char dashed from a small depression in the rock face, right between Tom and me. Though only a few feet from us, her coat blended so well with her surroundings that only her movement gave her away. Tom noted, "Given her speed and agility racing down the slope, I think she is in great condition."

It took a good five minutes for my heart rate and breathing to settle. We sat on the steep slope for awhile, reflecting on Char's fleeting image. The sight of a snow leopard in its natural world, a very un-catlike world, throttles the senses. One can't help but marvel at the only cat that adapted as two continents pushed upward for millions of years, evolving a body and spirit that thrives in high, lonely places. In just the last few thousand years, humans have learned to live among the great mountains, persistent in eking out a living as herders and farmers. Here in Mongolia, the most sparsely populated of the snow leopard countries, the question of coexistence remains unanswered. Tom's study hoped to reveal a basic understanding of the snow leopard so that parks and protected areas might be properly sized and conserved. Just knowing home ranges and movement patterns would help in drawing more meaningful protected area boundaries for a wide-ranging species like the snow leopard. Getting these data was the main reason George Schaller and Tserendeleg had set up the study.

From our resting spot up on the slope, we continued to scan for another look at Char. In the blink of an eye, she appeared among the boulders far below, then quietly disappeared, magically becoming part of the mountain.

Each day Tom tutored me in the art of snaring as we checked and reset some of the trap sites. The few free hours in the late afternoons were generally used to catch up on writing, mending clothes or equipment, and listening to music. One day a local herder came along, riding a massive Bactrian camel. The cowboy in me couldn't resist the offer to climb aboard. What wonderfully adapted beasts, elegantly ugly but beautifully suited for life in the desert: thick coat, long feminine eyelashes, and pan-sized feet. Up close they are huge, some over seven feet tall and weighing more than a ton. Marginal control over the beasts rests in a small pinky-sized piece of wood through the nasal septum, tied to a single lead line. Getting them to jackknife themselves up and down for loading requires persistence and deafness to the howls, wails, and moans that make you think the poor animal is in the last throes of death. It is hard not to like them in spite of their cantankerous nature. Sitting astride my woolly friend, thoughts of my horse, Princess, my little ranch, and my family surfaced. I was reminded that my time in the Gobi was drawing to an end.

It was hard to say goodbye to the boys. My time in the field went quickly. Snow leopard research is not a casual endeavor; it demands boot time, sweat, and precious time away from loved ones. We spoke little as the sun broke through the clouds, setting Mother Mountain ablaze in golden light. She looked reverent and serene, contented. It was long-shadow time in the Gobi; the rising sun cast spired shadows that stretched long behind desert sage, the landscape striped in remarkable hues of black and gold. I felt light and gifted, certain that this ageless scene had lifted the spirits of many before me. Like a scene from an old movie, we rumbled along in our little jeep awash in nature's shimmering splendor.

Tserendeleg met me at the airport and proffered an invitation to spend the night at his home: "Please, you stay at my house." I happily accepted. After we had unloaded my gear he took me to his office, where a fax from Annie awaited me with bad news. Tserendeleg handed me the faded page, which she had asked him to hold until my return from the field. My father had passed away quietly on February 21 in Livingston, Tennessee. I slumped into a chair beside Tserendeleg's desk, feeling drained, the weight of such news too heavy for tired legs. My friend stepped forward and with a reverent bow said, "I very sorry," then stepped back and held silent, his eyes conveying sincere sorrow and sympathy. I had known that Alzheimer's would eventually claim my father's life, but the actual happening, especially while I was so far away, caught me unprepared. I was moved that my family, knowing I could never make it to the funeral on time, had held the news so I could finish my fieldwork. On my third reading of the fax, it struck me like the cold wind of the Gobi that my dad's passing had coincided with the white light. I was confused. More of the Rat, or true cosmic synchrony?

Tserendeleg had a plan to help ease my sorrow. Cheerfully he said, "We go to Mongolian Opera tonight." I tried to quickly think of some way to defer gracefully, but inside I didn't want to be alone, especially since it was nighttime in Colorado; not a good time to wake my family. I cautiously accepted, not knowing how an opera might blend with my deepening sorrow. We hurried back to his house, where I tried to smooth out my cleanest dirty clothes for the event. I felt bad knowing that my ticket would normally have gone to Tserendeleg's wife. Through her son, she assured me of an outstanding conflict. I didn't buy it but agreed to go.

Outside the National Academic Theatre of Opera and Ballet of Mongolia, limousines carrying dignitaries, country flags fluttering atop front fenders, hinted that I was out of my element and woefully underdressed. The spectacular theater and beautifully dressed throng made me feel uneasy; I missed the big open night sky and solitude of the Gobi. It became clear that Tserendeleg was truly a national figure, as he received the salutations of top government officials and others of obvious means and influence. It is hard to recall and account for all the different feelings and emotions that waved through me at the time, but that evening moved me as much as my time in the Gobi, as much as any time in my life.

The theater darkened, subduing inglorious feelings beneath magnificent chandeliers. The evening's program honored Mongolia's seventy-fifth anniversary of independence from China. It featured the country's top artists in song, dance, and music. Spectacular operettas portrayed the long journey to independence, and there were many tributes to Genghis Khan, who was enjoying a revival throughout Mongolia. Like a sponge, I imbibed the marvelous sights and sounds—a stark contrast to Saksi Camp, a place with few modern conveniences. The setting, the electric sense of pride among the performers and audience, created a welcoming envelope in which I felt safe and warm, loosening emotions and thoughts deep within.

Slowly my body relaxed, conforming to the comfortable chair. As the operettas played out onstage before me, my mind mirrored another stage, my thoughts a slow procession of images: Tom McCarthy, good biologist and good father, granting me time to use my skills and stretch myself as a biologist; years of education and training put to good use; a career unfolding, passionate, exciting. I saw my father and me in scenes of life abundant on our little Tennessee farm. The mysterious and synchronized white light, what did it mean? Could it have been my father's spirit, his consciousness enveloped in a cosmic cloud twirling to a better place, a new beginning? Years later, after endless attempts at description, I discovered Rumi's precise abstraction of what I saw that February night:

> We come spinning out of nothingness
> Scattering stars like dust
>
> —RUMI

I also learned later that Mongolians, upon seeing a falling star, believe someone has died. Tradition calls for spitting over one's shoulder and saying with thanks, "It's not my star."

I thought of Logan, Jesse, Ben, and Annie; the hardship I cause them, the joy of family. Would they forgive my time away? Would they love me as I loved my father? And to sit with Tserendeleg, a man of great standing in his country, a man I respected, who made me feel good about what little difference we make toward greater, difficult aims such as protecting endangered animals. My heart wanted to float out of my body and join the great performance onstage. I was struck with strong feelings that sought release; tears welled in my eyes, finally bursting; small rivulets stained a dry, wind-hardened face—another unique, transcendent moment of joy, thanks, sorrow. I kept my head trained forward, a little embarrassed that Tserendeleg might find my emotional leakage awkward or think me an overly sensitive aficionado of Mongolian opera. Words cannot describe the emotional release of that moment.

That evening Tserendeleg's family helped me set aside my grief, comforting me once again with the warmth of their home and family interplay. We enjoyed a grand meal where again I felt the uniformity of life so clearly evident. Their home was like our home, a place of love and laughter, like most homes the world over. I felt blessed to be in Mongolia, to study a noble creature, to have had a loving father, and to have a loving family. The events of this trip would cut many ways, and it would take some time to process everything fully. Once again Homer's *Ulysses* came into my mind; the siren call to return home pulls from the same wellspring of emotion one experiences when anticipating a new journey. Internally, a new longing filled me. Some internal meter said it was time to go home, to the known. As on each trip before, I pondered whether my future held another journey, another chance to linger in the magic land of the snow leopard. A few months back, the same question had come up when I said goodbye to my Pakistani friend Ashiq. Like all questions of the future, his ageless response rang true. Enshallah.

R I N C H E N   W A N G C H U K

LEGENDS OF ZANSKAR

INDIA—*The snow leopard guides a native Ladakhi to safety and to a career in conservation.*

Once upon a time, there were three friends: a snow leopard, an otter, and a house cat. One fine day, after playing among themselves, they decided to partake of a special meal. "I will hunt a fat ibex on the far slope," said the snow leopard. The otter declared, "I will bring water from the river to quench our thirst." "I will bring fire from the nearby village for cooking our delicious meal," offered the house cat. Having decided so, the three went in separate directions. After much stalking, the snow leopard managed to kill a fat ibex. He then dragged the ibex carcass down the steep slope to the place where they were to meet. The otter, which had gone to fetch water from the river, came across a school of fish and became so absorbed chasing and playing with the fish that he forgot to return to the meeting spot. The house cat found the comforts of a house and stayed in the village relishing tasty butter and milk. The snow leopard waited and waited for his friends to return, then gave up and ate the ibex, leaving the spleen for the otter and the fat for the house cat. While the two friends never returned, to this day the snow leopard always leaves the spleen and fat of a kill for his friends, the otter and the house cat. So goes the legend from the Valley of Zanskar.

I grew up in the Valley of Nubra (Ldumra, or Valley of Flowers), listening to such beliefs and tales from our family's sheepherders — Tsering, Tundup, and Lhamo. Nubra lies north of Leh, the capital of Ladakh, India, and north of the Zanskar Mountains. To reach Nubra you must drive over Khardung La, the highest paved road on earth at 18,380 feet. Most of the people in our valley were agriculturists, but my family raised livestock. Collectively, we cared for about 130 sheep and goats, enough for a comfortable livelihood in Nubra. Only my bride's family owned more. My family name, Stakrey, was conferred on one of my ancestors by the king of Ladakh in honor of his fierceness in battle, beating back raiders from Tibet. Stakrey means "tiger-like." My father followed in the warrior path, joining the Indo-Pakistan conflict at age seventeen and becoming one of India's most highly decorated soldiers. It would seem that my fate was to become a soldier as well, but, as it turned out, my life path would be influenced not by war but instead by a wild creature of Ladakhi lore and early childhood memories.

As children, my cousin and I would follow the herd as it lazily grazed among the brush. At the onset of winter we would take our livestock across the frozen Nubra River to graze all day on the thickets of sea-buck forest. In places the thicket would allow only narrow paths and at times would become so entangled that we would have to retrace our footsteps to get back to an open spot. Occasionally, we would come across a lynx track. Tsering would warn us to take special care of the younger sheep and goats, as lynx were notorious stock killers. Our vigil of protection included other predators such as red fox, wolves, and — the most elusive of them all — the snow leopard.

One cold winter day it had snowed during the morning before we set out to cross the river. In the deep thicket, my cousin Skalzang and I followed a fresh lynx track until it disappeared into thick brush. Later we rejoined Tsering and the herd near the foothill. With the sun high overhead, Tsering started a noontime fire and began the ritual of making our lunch of tea and stew. Skalzang and I were collecting wood for the fire when suddenly all the sheep panicked and began running helter-skelter. We overheard Tsering cursing and saw him pelting stones at a bush a few yards away. After awhile we realized that the predator had taken one of the goats. Blood stained the trail leading into the brush; pieces of goat hair stuck to the thorns of the sea buck marked its path as well. We tried following the tracks, assuming they were those of a large lynx. Its pugmarks led us to the base of a hill, then they disappeared up and over a rugged rock outcrop. We scanned the steep terrain for signs of this stealthy cat, finding clues of neither the predator nor its prey. Looking more closely at the rocky outcrop, we couldn't imagine the cat carrying the fat goat up such a steep slope, so we began retracing our steps, looking for the carcass. For another hour we looked and looked but found nothing. Tsering concluded that "the culprit was not a lynx but rather a snow leopard, the only predator capable of carrying such a heavy load up the steep rock face." He added, "Legend has it [that] the snow leopard can carry prey balanced on its back with its long tail wrapped tight around."

In the fall of 1990, at age twenty-one, I was part of an expedition to Mount Saser Kangri II (24,606 feet in elevation), pursuing my ambition at the time to become a mountaineering guide. For most of a day we struggled to get across a glacier full of crevices, without success, when we came across animal tracks heading in the direction we needed to go. Seeing that the tracks were those of a snow leopard, my mind flooded with childhood memories. Trusting the cat's good instinct, knowing that it thrives in the land of snow and ice and rock, we began following its tracks, dug deep into the melting ice. Its pugmarks zigged and zagged over the glacier and leaped over several minor depressions in the ice, some leaps covering distances of fifteen to twenty feet. The cat's apprehension at these points became our apprehension, even though we were properly roped. Sure enough, when we tested these depressions, they actually hid deep crevices. For nearly five miles we followed tracks through the glacier, safely reaching the other side. To our amazement, two sets of tracks continued on from that point. We were delighted to find we had been trailing two cats, one walking in perfect precision behind the other. Our excitement at following two cats temporarily subdued our euphoria over having been led across a dangerous glacier by the elusive snow leopard. If only they could have warned us of the danger above.

After leaving the aegis of our big cats, the climb became very difficult, and a sheer rock face separated us from the final summit push. After we completed this arduous climb, a member of our party began to talk and act strangely, certain signs of cerebral edema. His condition worsened, so we decided to descend with him to Camp Four. His delirium led to careless climbing—he fell to his death despite our concerted efforts to help him navigate the steep terrain. The subzero temperatures continued to hamper our descent. That cold mountain took a climbing partner and four of my toes. It also took my passion for climbing mountains as a profession. In the hospital, my father told me that the loss of my toes would prohibit a life in the military. In truth, I was relieved, having never felt drawn to such a life; rather, my heart seemed more aligned with the teachings of Gandhi. Fate or kismet had deepened my love of mountains, and the spirit animal of my youth would continue to weave in and out of my life.

Good fortune granted me both a friendship with Chering Norbu, the district forest officer for Ladakh, and a government post with responsibility to protect all of Ladakh's forests and wildlife. Norbu was a good friend of my father's and a truly wonderful human being, and his knowledge and caring for wildlife were legendary, as I learned when he came to visit and told stories over a glass of whiskey. He graciously shared all that he knew about wildlife and taught me the snow leopard's habits and signs, such as scrapes, pugmarks, and scent rocks. Armed with a greater understanding of, and respect for, this rare cat, I began leading treks and documentary filmmakers into the mountains surrounding Ladakh in search of the mythical cat. From these experiences a new ambition that called for greater involvement in snow leopard conservation arose inside me. I wanted to become more involved but didn't know how. More kismet. Rodney Jackson was visiting

Ladakh, looking for partners in snow leopard conservation. He not only taught me more about snow leopards, but he also hired me as a local partner. I could not believe my good fortune: getting paid to help the snow leopard, a job I had volunteered to do. In addition to Rodney, I got to know Raghu Chundawat, a research fellow from the Wildlife Institute of India, who was studying sheep and the snow leopard in Hemis National Park, just south of Leh in the Zanskar Mountains. Like Rodney, Raghu freely shared his knowledge of snow leopards, adding greatly to my understanding of this rare cat of my homeland.

Within a short time, my treks featured the snow leopard, and my new post with the Snow Leopard Trust allowed me to work directly with local people to find new ways for humans and the snow leopard to coexist. Just a few years later, with the direct involvement of local villagers, I helped start a "home stay" program that lets trekkers stay over in local homes. Trekkers love the interaction with local people, and participants gain much-appreciated income in exchange for protecting the snow leopard.

Like my childhood, my adult life has been blessed by memorable encounters with a native cat that seems to have chosen me, directing my path in life. When I led a group of Earthwatch volunteers into Hemis National Park, we were to count blue sheep under the watchful eye of Dr. Joe Fox, a professor at the University of Tromsø. Camped close to a marmot colony at about 16,000 feet elevation, the volunteers had fanned out to comb the hillside, counting burrows. I held back at a vantage point, scanning surrounding slopes for wildlife. Suddenly, I chanced upon two cats running across the steep slope across the valley. Two lynx playing, I thought, but the distance was too great to be certain. I scrambled quickly back to camp to fetch the spotting scopes, but when I returned I couldn't immediately relocate the cats. Cursing my luck, I continued to scan until I finally located them father up the mountain. They were not lynx but instead a large snow leopard with a smaller sub-adult. I yelled, "Snow leopard!" Soon, the entire camp gathered around two spotting scopes, marveling at the sight of these magnificent cats.

That evening the volunteers, in a particularly festive mood, recounted their excitement about actually seeing a snow leopard in the wild. But our horseman had an entirely different view. For him, the sighting of cats so near was worrisome; he feared a nighttime attack on his ponies that would inflict economic hardship. Tsering's warning voice from my childhood rang in my ears as I lay awake thinking about the two perspectives on today's snow leopard sighting. For the visitors, a glimpse of such an elusive and majestic cat marked a high point in their lives. For the horseman and local villagers, the snow leopard evoked fear and contempt. These conflicting views filled my mind as I lay beneath a star-filled sky. Was there a way to resolve this age-old conflict between local people and the snow leopard? Will the home stay program work long-term? What legends shall I tell my children? As I pondered these questions, I could hear the horseman awake, his vigil into the night just beginning.

HELEN FREEMAN

MAGIC VALLEY

QOMOLONGMA—*The world's highest mountain heeds the call for help as danger invades the peaceful valley of the snow leopard. This is only a fairy tale, but then, who knows? As the song says, "Fairy tales can come true . . ."*

They had lived in the valley for a thousand years. They knew what life had been like before they had come to this isolated region because the Old Ones had told them. Before was a time of eternal ice, when the world was frozen and the air was filled with dread and endless cold. Now the sun had returned, and although snow stayed on the mountain peaks, in the spring streams flowed and flowers filled the meadow.

They were the snow leopards, and this was their Magic Valley.

The first snow leopards that had come to the valley had grown old and gone up to the shining palace in the sky. Other snow leopards had stepped in and become the leaders. This story is about one such couple, Igor and Maria.

One day, after patrolling the boundaries of his range, Igor walked up a steep talus slope to his favorite lookout. He lay down on a flat boulder, gave a long yawn, and rested his head on his massive paws. Maria, his mate, arrived at the same time. She gave him a gentle head rub to say how pleased she was to see him. Igor responded by blowing little puffs of air through his nostrils. It was a soft sound, the greeting call of the snow leopard. Maria looked into his eyes and made the same soft little noise back to him. They snuggled together, their tails touching.

Both of them had reached this place silently, for when a snow leopard walks, it is as if a feather has brushed the ground. Mountains appreciate this gentleness. One mountain will often remark to another how special it feels to have a snow leopard pad across its back. "A little to the left," the mountain will say. "There's a bit of an itch there, and it would feel so good if you could just walk across it."

But the mountains save their biggest smiles for when the cubs come out to play. Snow leopard paws are huge, and cubs have a hard time keeping them under control. Cubs often walk as if their feet were encased in moon boots. They slip off rocks and their steps squash and squish. Then there is the problem of their tails. Their tails, which are longer than all the rest of their body put together, are the absolutely perfect example of how one part of the body can have a mind of its own.

For example, let's say a cub thinks it is big and scary and can catch anything. It drops to the ground, belly flat, paws tucked under, and moves forward ever so slowly toward the prey. But the tail immediately thrusts itself straight up in the air, waves like a flag, and gives away every step of the approach.

On this particular afternoon in the life of Igor and Maria, a blur of fur came tumbling out from behind a bush and slid down the slope, just missing them. It was their two youngest cubs, Pushkin and Nicholas. Their older sister, Irina, was sunbathing on a nearby rock. She tossed her head back and with a flick of her tail (which she had only recently learned to bring under her control) said, "Goodness, Mother, can't you tell them to be more quiet?"

And as she always did, her mother answered, "Boys will be boys, my dear."

And so time passed happily in the valley of the snow leopards. But nothing can last forever. Danger came to Magic Valley because the Outsiders discovered the secret of snow leopard fur. They had found that to touch snow leopard fur was to know the caress of a cloud. They knew they could sell such fur for much money.

One day Qomolongma, the highest mountain of them all, felt a strange stomping across its range. It was not the familiar tread of a villager setting out to chop wood. It was much heavier and very menacing. She asked the other mountains if they knew what it was. When the question got to little Namcha, the closest mountain to the land of the Outsiders, they learned the answer.

"It is the bad hunters," she said. "They have killed all the animals that used to live on me, and now they want to find the snow leopards of Magic Valley. They want their fur."

The mountains did not want to lose their snow leopards. "What can we do?" said one. "Let us ask Igor and Maria," replied Qomolongma.

So that is how it came to pass that Igor and Maria left the cubs with Irina and walked out of their Magic Valley. As they leaped from peak to peak they told their plan to each mountain, and every mountain, big or small, said it would do its best.

By now the hunters, heavily loaded with guns and poisoned spears, had made great headway toward the valley. They were as close as Qomolongma. That was when they first saw Igor. He was standing on a ridge and his tail was high in the air, flashing back and forth as if to say, "Follow me!" The leader of the hunters yelled to some of his men to go after Igor. "Catch and kill!" he screamed.

Igor fell behind a rock and waited for the killers. As they came over the ridge, he softly padded three times on the slope. From inside the mountain came a rumbling. Igor immediately made a giant leap to the next mountain. The Outsiders could not move fast enough. "Avalanche!" they cried. But it was too late: a giant wall of snow came down and they perished.

The other hunters heard the rumbling but did not pay any attention. Instead their eyes were on Maria, who was casually walking up a rocky face, seductively waving the tip of her tail back and forth.

"Let's get her," yelled the leader, and all the men followed him onto the steep hillside of stone. With three taps of her furry paw

Maria signaled, and the mountain shook as hard as it could. Maria gave a mighty lunge and leaped forward, over the tons of jagged rocks now rolling down the slope toward her. She made it to a high ridge. But the Outsiders could not escape, and all of them were crushed by the mountain's fury.

People say the bad Outsiders have stopped looking for the Magic Valley because they think it is too dangerous, not worth dying for, and probably only a myth anyway. But the snow leopards know it is real. It is their home.

If you are a kind person and love animals, you may be lucky enough to find the Magic Valley. There you will discover a land where snow leopards play and mountains smile. I should tell you, though, that it will be a very hard journey. But I should also tell you that it is well worth the effort.

ORGANIZATIONS AND RELATED WEBSITES

INTERNATIONAL CONSERVATION ORGANIZATIONS

Altai Conservancy: altaiconservancy.org
Cat Action Treasury: felidae.org
Conservation International: conservation.org
Defenders of Wildlife: defenders.org
Felidae Conservation Fund: felidaefund.org
Flora and Fauna International: fauna-flora.org
International Exotic Animal Sanctuary: bigcat.org
International Union for Conservation of Nature: iucn.org
IUCN Cat Specialist Group: catsg.org
Mountain Institute: mountain.org
NABU (German-language site): nabu.de/themen/international/laender/
    kirgistan
National Geographic Society: nationalgeographic.com
Nature Conservancy—Yunnan, China, Project: nature.org/
    wherewework/asiapacific/china/work
Pacific Environment: pacificenvironment.org
Panthera Foundation: panthera.org

Plateau Perspectives: plateauperspectives.org
Snow Leopard Conservancy: snowleopardconservancy.org
Snow Leopard Network: snowleopardnetwork.org
Snow Leopard Network Blog: snowleopardnetwork.org/blog/
Snow Leopard Trust: snowleopard.org
Wildlife Conservation Society: wcs.org
Wildlife Watch Group: citesnepal.org
Woodland Park Zoo: zoo.org
World Wide Fund for Nature: worldwildlife.org
World Wildlife Fund–UK: wwf.org/uk

SNOW LEOPARD RANGE STATE NON-GOVERNMENTAL ORGANIZATIONS AND AGENCIES

Altai Foundation (English-language site): altaiconservancy.org
Asia Irbis (Russian-language site): asia-irbis.narod.ru
Department of National Parks and Wildlife Conservation (Nepal): dnpwc.
    gov.np
Environmental Protection Society: eps-swat.org
International Centre for Integrated Mountain Development: icimod.org
King Mahendra Trust for Nature Conservation (Nepal): ntnc.org.np
Mongolian Association for the Conservation of Nature and Environment:
    owc.org.mn/macne
Nature Conservation Foundation (India): ncf-india.org
Snowlands Great River Association (China): snowland-great-rivers.org
Wildlife Institute of India: wwi.gov.in
Wildlife of Pakistan: wildlifeofpakistan.com
Wildlife Protection Society of India: wpsi-india.org
World Wildlife Fund–Bhutan: wwfbuhtan.org.bt
World Wildlife Fund–China: wwfchina.org
World Wildlife Fund–India: wwfindia.org
World Wildlife Fund–Mongolia: www.wwf.mn
World Wildlife Fund–Nepal: wwfnepal.org
World Wildlife Fund–Pakistan: wwfpak.org
World Wildlife Fund–Russia: www.wwf.ru
Xinjiang Conservation Fund (China): greenxinjiang.org

OTHER CONSERVATION ORGANIZATIONS AND RESOURCES

Audubon Naturalist Society: audubonnaturalist.org

Big Cats Online: dialspace.dial.pipex.com

Biodiversity Hotspots: biodiversityhotspots.org

Carnivore Conservation and Ecology Portal: carnivoreconservation.org

Central Park Zoo: centralparkzoo.com

China Green Times (Chinese-language site): greentimes.com

CITES: cites.org

Houston Zoo: houstonzoo.org

Padmaja Naidu Himalayan Zoological Park in Darjeeling: pnhzp.gov.in

Rocky Mountain Cat Conservancy: catconservancy.org

San Francisco Zoo: sfzoo.org

Saving Snow Leopards Blog: snowleopardblog.com

TRAFFIC: traffic.org

United States Fish and Wildlife Service: fws.gov

Wildlife Conservation Network: wildnet.org

FURTHER READING

Hillard, Darla. *Vanishing Tracks*. Boyne City, MI: Arbor, 1990.

Johnston, Marianne. *Snow Leopards and Their Babies*. New York: PowerKids, 1999.

Landau, Elaine. *Snow Leopards: Hunters of Snow and Ice*. Berkeley Heights, NJ: Enslow Elementary, 2010.

Matthiessen, Peter. *The Snow Leopard*. New York: Bantam Books, 1978.

Montgomery, Sy. *Saving the Ghost of the Mountain*. Wilmington, MA: Houghton Mifflin Harcourt, 2009.

Morris, Jackie. *The Snow Leopard*. London: Francis Lincoln Children's Books, 2007.

Radcliffe, Theresa. *The Snow Leopard*. London: Puffin Books, 1996.

BIOGRAPHICAL NOTES

Ali Abutalip Dahashof was born into a small pastoralist family that raised sheep on the edge of the Qinghai-Tibetan Plateau. With five siblings and parents consumed with work, he became self-reliant at a young age. At age five he began riding horseback, helping his father with herding, and learning from him Kazak history and culture. At ten he began attending school. Though challenged by the Chinese language, he studied hard and went on to middle school, graduating with honors. In 1983 he was chosen to attend the affiliated high school of the Central Minorities Institute in Beijing and again graduated with honors, achieving the highest score of any Kazak student in Aksai County on the nationwide college entrance examination. This enabled him to enroll in the Grassland Department of Gansu Agricultural University in Lanzhou, where he obtained an associate degree. In July 1989 he returned to his homeland and a few years later joined the Aksai County Wild Fauna and Flora Protection Station. Ali has participated in two international conferences on wild camels and published "Wild Camel Resources of Annanba Nature Reserve, Aksai Kazak Autonomous County" and "Water Resources and Wild Camels." In 2007 he represented Gansu Province at the international symposium on snow leopards in Beijing. Since 1998, he and Dr. Richard B. Harris of the University of Montana have conducted research on the argali sheep population in the Kharteng Valley of Aksai County. He and Dr. Harris have coauthored scientific papers on their study.

Som B. Ale, PhD, is a postdoctoral research associate at the University of Minnesota, Department of Fisheries, Wildlife, and Conservation Biology. His research will identify and delineate snow leopard corridors that connect protected areas in Nepal's mountains that harbor snow leopards. His study will lead to better protection of snow leopards in valleys outside Nepal's protected areas.

Avaantseren Bayarjargal is the founder and executive director of the Snow Leopard Conservation Foundation (SLCF). The SLCF works closely with the Snow Leopard Trust and implements its conservation and research programs in Mongolia. She holds a master's degree from Kimmage Development Studies Centre in Ireland. Bayara developed a conservation program now known as Snow Leopard Enterprises (SLE). This community-based model allows poor semi-nomadic herders to increase their income through handicraft production in exchange for community tolerance of snow leopards that commonly prey on livestock. The SLE program has grown to include twenty-six communities, helping more than 400 herder families. Bayara was awarded the 2009 Rabinowitz-Kaplan Prize for the Next Generation in Wild Cat Conservation.

Yash Veer Bhatnagar, PhD, directs the Snow Leopard Trust's India Program and is a senior scientist with the Nature Conservation Foundation. He has been involved with research and conservation of the snow leopard and its prey species in the Himalayan regions of India for nearly two decades. His main areas of interest are snow leopard and prey status and distribution in India, their ecology, and the design and implementation of robust conservation programs at the community, state government, and central government levels. Dr. Bhatnagar supervises studies on mitigating conflicts between snow leopards and people, snow leopards' diet, and snow leopard monitoring; he also trains field personnel in snow leopard monitoring techniques. An important engagement for the past few years has been to bring stakeholders together to discuss modalities of developing a national strategy and action plan for conserving the Indian high altitudes, keeping the snow leopard as a flagship species. These efforts have led to the initiation of Project Snow Leopard in the country, a participatory program sponsored by the Ministry of Environment and Forests, Government of India.

Joseph L. Fox, PhD, began his conservation career in Asia in the early 1970s through the US Peace Corps, working for the National Parks Department in Nepal. For nearly forty years his research and teaching have focused on large-mammal ecology and conservation in the Himalaya Mountains and the Tibetan Plateau. For twenty years he taught ecology and conservation biology at the University of Tromsø, Norway, and he is currently an independent consultant and adjunct faculty member at Western State College in Colorado. He continues to work on wildlife-related projects, including the snow leopard, in Tibetan areas of China from his home base in Lake City, Colorado.

Helen Freeman founded the Snow Leopard Trust (SLT) in 1981 as a nongovernmental, nonprofit organization dedicated solely to snow leopard conservation. She remained active in SLT activities until her death in 2007. Her chapters in this volume, "Kashmir" and "Magic Valley," are from her memoir, *Life, Laughter, and the Pursuit of Snow Leopards.* Helen helped or worked directly with the majority of the authors in this book. In addition to possessing an unbridled passion for snow leopards, she was a wonderful and giving human being sorely missed by all who knew her.

Rich Harris received an MS in wildlife biology in 1984 and a PhD in wildlife management from the University of Montana in 1993. He has worked for the US Fish and Wildlife Service as a caribou biologist in Alaska and for the state of Montana's Forest Management Bureau as a wildlife biologist. In western China, since 1988 he has worked with provincial and university personnel in Qinghai, Gansu, Xinjiang, Yunnan, and Inner Mongolia on wildlife survey and conservation issues. He has also conducted research on mountain ungulates in Afghanistan and Mongolia. His book *Wildlife Conservation in China: Preserving the Habitat of China's Wild West* was published in the United States in 2007 by M. E. Sharpe and in China in 2010 by China Environmental Sciences Press. He is an adjunct associate professor of wildlife conservation in the Department of Ecosystem and Conservation Sciences at the University of Montana in Missoula.

Darla Hillard is co-director of the Snow Leopard Conservancy (SLC), having spent thirty years working with her partner, Rodney Jackson, to save snow leopards. She manages the SLC office, oversees fundraising, and directs small-scale field-based conservation education activities while still finding time to write. She co-wrote the June 1986 *National Geographic* cover article, followed by the book *Vanishing Tracks: Four Years among the Snow Leopards of Nepal.* "On the Trail of Wild Snow Leopards," one of two articles

Darla has written for the widely read *Highlights for Children*, was chosen Science Feature of 1994. She has also written for *Summit* and *Bay Nature* magazines and contributed to the anthology *Travelers Tales: San Francisco.*

Don Hunter, PhD, received his doctorate in ecology from Colorado State University. His career has taken a dual track in technology and ecology. As technologist, he headed a team of information technology specialists that developed Web-based support systems and tested new technologies, such as computer mapping systems and satellite telemetry. As ecologist, his studies in central Asia focused on mountain biodiversity conservation and collaborative research on the endangered snow leopard. His work with snow leopards in central Asia compliments his research on mountain lions in Rocky Mountain National Park. He is science director for the Rocky Mountain Cat Conservancy (www.catconservancy.org), a nongovernmental, nonprofit organization dedicated to wild cat conservation worldwide. He writes and continues to work on snow leopard conservation from his home in Bellvue, Colorado.

Shafqat Hussain, PhD, is an assistant professor in the Department of Anthropology at Trinity College in Hartford, Connecticut. He has worked on snow leopard conservation in Pakistan since 1998, when he helped set up Project Snow Leopard in the Baltistan region of northern Pakistan. His work in snow leopard conservation is driven by an academic pursuit and his personal love of the immense mountains of high Asia. Dr. Hussain holds a PhD in anthropology and environmental studies from Yale University.

Rodney Jackson, PhD, is founder-director of the Snow Leopard Conservancy. He brings thirty years of hands-on experience to the work of advancing community-based stewardship of the snow leopard through education, research, and grassroots conservation action. He is widely recognized as the leading expert on snow leopards. He conducted the first in-depth study of the cats in the 1980s, served as the Snow Leopard Trust's first conservation director, prepared the snow leopard section of the International Union for Conservation of Nature (IUCN)–World Conservation Union's Status Survey and Conservation Action Plan for Cats, and sits on the IUCN's Cat Specialist Core Group. He is an honorary fellow of the California Academy of Sciences

Jan E. Janecka, PhD, is a wildlife biologist focusing on conservation genetics, population genetics, and the evolution of mammalian diversity. He received a PhD from Texas A&M University in 2006 and currently holds a postdoctoral research associate position there. He works closely with the Snow Leopard Conservancy (SLC), Irbis Mongolia, and the Mongolian Academy of Sciences. He contributed to the 2008 International Snow Leopard Conference and has published articles on snow leopards in the journals *Cat News* and *Animal Conservation*. He is also an associate of the SLC and a member of the IUCN Cat Specialist Group and the Snow Leopard Network.

Evgeniy P. Kashkarov, PhD, was born in western Siberia in the city of Stalinsk (today Novokuznetsk, Kemerovsky region). In 1980 he received a master's degree in biology from Irkutsk State University and in 1992 was awarded a PhD in biogeography from Moscow State University. From 1981 to 1993 he was affiliated with the Tien Shan High Mountain Station of the Academy of Science, Kirgizia. He conducted research on the snow leopard in Siberia and Mongolia, the northernmost marginal areas of the snow leopard's range. He often collaborates with the Snow Leopard Trust. His last project with the Klickitat Organics partnership in the Russian Far East and Trans-Baikal-Altai dealt with the protection of Amur tiger, Amur leopard, and snow leopard migration corridors. He has published more than eighty articles, including a 1989 monograph *Snow Leopard in Kirgizia*. His current focus is the reconstruction of Pleistocene mammals' Ice Age history and nature conservation issues.

Mitchell Kelly studied zoology and botany at the University of Western Australia and then earned a degree in film and television from Curtin University. He has been a wildlife documentary cinematographer since 1992. He prefers animal-behavior films, specializing in rare and elusive animals in inaccessible, difficult areas. From 1999 to 2003 he spent four winters and three summers in the trans-Himalayan region of Ladakh shooting two films featuring wild snow leopards: "Wild Asia: At the Edge" (for the Discovery Channel) — from which his story comes — and "Silent Roar: Searching for the Snow Leopard" (for WNET, screened on PBS). Since then he has lectured and presented screenings at snow leopard fundraising and awareness-raising events in the United States, New Zealand, and Australia. His films are used in Ladakh to educate both locals and tourists about the region's snow leopards and other wildlife. He plans to make a third snow leopard film about the conservation issues that are determining the leopard's future. Kelly lives in Perth, Western Australia.

Ashiq Ahmad Khan was born in 1947 and holds masters degrees in zoology and forestry from the University of Peshawar, Pakistan, and a master's degree in natural resource management from the University of Edinburgh, United Kingdom. He served as a wildlife management specialist at the Pakistan Forest Institute until 1992. He has held the posts of conservation director and chief technical adviser for the Worldwide Fund for Nature–Pakistan. Khan is a member of several professional committees, including the IUCN's Cat Specialist Group. His current engagements and associations include member, Advisory Board, Ministry of Environment, Government of Pakistan; special adviser, World Wildlife Fund–Pakistan; member, National Council for the Conservation of Wildlife; visiting professor, Sinkiong Institute of Ecology and Geography, Urumqi-China; associate editor-in-chief, *Journal of Arid Lands*, Chinese Academy of Sciences; chairman, Steering Committee, Snow Leopard Network; and chairman, Steering Committee, Pak-China Collaboration for Conservation and Sustainable Development. The author of more than fifty publications on various aspects of ecology and the general environment, Khan recently developed a Strategic Plan for the Conservation of Snow Leopards in Pakistan that has been approved by the government of Pakistan.

Nasier A. Kitchloo is the wildlife warden for Kashmir, India. While serving as chief wildlife warden for Ladakh, Kitchloo raised a snow leopard, Sheru, which was eventually moved to Padmaja Naidu Himalayan Zoological Park. Kitchloo was raised in Kashmir, India, and received training in wildlife management from various Indian universities. He has traveled widely, augmenting his education and experience in protected area management and rare species conservation.

Peter Matthiessen published *The Snow Leopard* in 1978, bringing worldwide attention to the mystical cat of central Asia's high mountains and critical acclaim to Peter. *The Snow Leopard* earned him the National Book Award in 1980 and set a high standard for modern nature writing. Drawn from a world of awe and wonder, his works evoke sincere compassion for our environment and the human condition. His latest work, *Shadow Country*, earned Peter his second National Book Award in 2008.

Kyle McCarthy, PhD, began his association with wildlife at an early age. When he was a child, his family moved to Admiralty Island, Alaska, where his father conducted research on brown bear food habits. Since then, he has been working with wildlife in one way or another, from capturing snow leopards with his father in the Altai Mountains of Mongolia to collaring the first golden cat in Sumatra with his wife. Dr. McCarthy received his bachelor's degree in wildlife biology from Colorado State University

(CSU), where as a student he also worked for the Biological Resource Management Division of the National Park Service. Most important, at CSU he met his wife, a fellow nature lover and now a peer in the wildlife conservation field. They moved to Massachusetts to pursue more education. He completed an MS on snow leopard populations in the Tien Shan Mountains of Kyrgyzstan and a PhD on common loons in New Hampshire. He is fascinated by all wildlife but holds a special place in his heart for the snow leopard. He and his wife are currently working on wild felids in Indonesia, and he continues to be an active member of the snow leopard community. He has published work on snow leopards in the *Journal of Wildlife Biology* and *Cat News* and has made presentations to various peer groups and general audiences.

Tom McCarthy, PhD, began his professional career studying brown bear, black bear, mountain goats, and caribou in Alaska in the early 1980s. A strong interest in international conservation led him to Mongolia in 1992, where he assumed management of a long-term snow leopard research project under the guidance of Dr. George B. Schaller. The six-year study was the basis for his PhD at the University of Massachusetts–Amherst, during which he became the first person to use satellite radio-collars on the cats. In addition to snow leopards, he conducted groundbreaking studies on wild camels and Gobi brown bears, two of Mongolia's rarest animals. He became the science and conservation director of the Snow Leopard Trust (SLT) in 2000 and has since led the organization's extensive science and community-based conservation programs across much of the snow leopard range in Asia. He has helped establish projects in Afghanistan, Bhutan, China, India, Kyrgyzstan, Mongolia, and Pakistan. Dr. McCarthy also serves as executive director of the Snow Leopard Network, a global consortium of more than 200 professionals involved in snow leopard research and conservation. In July 2008 Dr. McCarthy became the director of Snow Leopard Programs for the Panthera Foundation, a new nongovernmental organization dedicated to wild cat conservation. He continues to maintain a leadership role with the SLT. Recently, Dr. McCarthy and Dr. Schaller again selected Mongolia as the site for snow leopard research and launched the first-ever long-term intensive study of the endangered cats. This program, a collaborative program of Panthera and the SLT, will provide unprecedented scientific information necessary for effective conservation of snow leopards range-wide. In 2010 he was awarded the State of Mongolia Friendship Medal, the highest state award given to a foreign civilian, for his contribution to wildlife conservation.

George B. Schaller, PhD, is a field biologist with and vice president of the Panthera Foundation and senior conservationist with the Wildlife Conservation Society, both based in New York. He was born in 1933 and did his undergraduate work at the University of Alaska and graduate work at the University of Wisconsin. Dr. Schaller has spent most of his time in the field in Asia, Africa, and South America, studying and helping protect animals as diverse as the mountain gorilla, jaguar, giant panda, tiger, lion, and wild sheep and goats of the Himalaya. These animals have been the basis for his scientific and popular writings, including sixteen books—among them *The Year of the Gorilla, The Serengeti Lion, The Last Panda,* and *Tibet's Hidden Wilderness.* Dr. Schaller has worked for nearly two decades on the Tibetan Plateau in collaboration with Chinese and Tibetan scientists studying the wildlife—such as Tibetan antelope, wild yak, and snow leopard—and working on behalf of its survival. In addition, in recent years he has conducted conservation projects in Laos, Myanmar, Mongolia, Iran, Tajikistan, and other countries. His awards include the International Cosmos Prize (Japan), the Tyler Prize for Environmental Achievement (United States), and the Indianapolis Prize (United States).

Rinchen Wangchuk was program director of the Snow Leopard Conservancy (SLC)–India. In March 2011 Rinchen succumbed to Motor Neuron Disease just months after completing his story, *Legends of Zanskar.* Based in Leh, Ladakh, he worked closely with livestock-herding communities to predator-proof nighttime corrals. He trained local people, especially women and young men, in ways to enhance their income-generation skills through activities closely linked to the conservation of snow leopards. He also assisted local nongovernmental organizations in protecting India's rich mountain biodiversity. Rinchen was responsible for rural tourism initiatives under an acclaimed United Nations Educational, Scientific, and Cultural Organization–sponsored project that enabled SLC and its partners to launch the award-winning Himalayan Home Stay Program. His commitment to the welfare of both wildlife and rural people grew out of his Ladakhi village upbringing and his experiences as a skilled mountaineer and nature tour guide. With fellow Indian climbers he summited the 24,660-foot Saser Kangri II in Ladakh's Nubra region. He received special training in community-based tourism from the Mountain Institute (Nepal) and RECROFT (Thailand). He also helped develop the Earthwatch program Land of the Snow Leopard. He served as naturalist and field assistant on several documentaries, including the widely acclaimed *Silent Roar: Searching for the Snow Leopard.*

ILLUSTRATION CREDITS

Range map — Snow Leopard Conservancy

Karimabad, capital of Hunza, northern Pakistan — Don Hunter

Breaking camp, western China — Don Hunter

Snow leopard tracks — Rodney Jackson

Snow leopard cheek-rubbing — Steve Winter

Ashiq Ahmad Kahn talking with local Chitrali, Pakistan — Don Hunter

Snow leopard in snow, Ladakh, India — Rodney Jackson

Remote fieldwork, Mongolia — Jan Janecka

Snow leopard at night in the snow — Steve Winter

Snow leopard scent-spraying — Steve Winter

Snow leopard in snow — Rodney Jackson

Snow leopard and two cubs — Rodney Jackson

Chhimi Gurgung with villagers — Rodney Jackson

Nubra herder, leopard-proof corral — Snow Leopard Conservancy

ILLUSTRATION CREDITS

Snow leopard, showing long tail—Steve Winter

Prayer flags, Ladakh, India—Don Hunter

Snow leopard walking by remote camera in snow—Rodney Jackson

Snow leopard walking—Steve Winter

Nicholas and Alexandra—Snow Leopard Trust and Helen Freeman

Snow leopard walking toward camera—Steve Winter